REDEMPTION ROAD

'If you want to know what it is like to set out on a journey of bereavement, if you want to know how suicide affects a person, if you want to know what it feels like to find some healing, then this is the book for you. Brendan writes beautifully and evocatively about his brother Donal, and the lengths that he goes to (the end of the world) for him. I couldn't recommend it highly enough.'
Paul Kelly, CEO and founder of Console

'*Redemption Road* tells the story of a Jesuit walking the Camino and grappling with living his faith after the tragic death of his brother. His developing comprehension of the massive encompassing reality of God's constant presence at all times and in all places, through the working out of his Jesuit spirituality in moments of immense joy and agonising pain, is faithfully told. It speaks with great integrity and honesty about the journey from desolation to peace. This is a journal of hope.'
Baroness Nuala O'Loan, former Police Ombudsman for Northern Ireland

'Brendan McManus's profoundly moving memoir of his journey to wholeness and healing after his brother's suicide is a standout. He takes the reader along on a physical pilgrimage, but also on a remarkable journey of reconciliation, grace and, ultimately, peace. *Redemption Road* moved me deeply, and I'm proud of my brother Jesuit for sharing with us his honest and heartfelt story.'
James Martin SJ, Jesuit priest, editor of America *magazine and author of several award-winning books*

'In this beautiful book Brendan McManus shares with us the authentic story of his journey on the Camino. Through his experiences along the ancient route he comes to understand the process of his own transformation, as a modern-day pilgrim moving away from despair, searching for the restoration of his faith in hope and love.'
Dr Jim Lucey, psychiatrist and medical director of St Patrick's University Hospital

'Brendan McManus has written a very vivid and absorbing account of his personal pilgrimage on the Camino to Santiago de Compostela. Riveting and intense; this is no walk in the park, but an invitation to see Ignatian discernment in action and to accompany a grieving man going through great darkness to light. It is a great read.'
Fr William A. Barry SJ, distinguished US spiritual director and author

'In my work as a broadcaster I have too often witnessed the grief and despair of those who have lost a loved one through death by suicide. So it is truly heartening to read of Brendan's odyssey on the Camino and his courageous message of hope. He writes as someone who knows the pain of loss but is able to find a way through – an expression of the suffering that has an 11th hour deliverance. This book lifted my heart and I'm sure it will bring great solace to those bereaved as he was.'
Miriam O'Callaghan, Broadcaster, RTE

REDEMPTION ROAD

Grieving on the Camino

Brendan McManus SJ

ORPEN PRESS

Published by
Orpen Press
Lonsdale House
Avoca Avenue
Blackrock
Co. Dublin
Ireland

e-mail: info@orpenpress.com
www.orpenpress.com

Paperback ISBN 978-1-909895-39-3
ePub ISBN 978-1-909895-43-0
Kindle ISBN 978-1-909895-44-7
PDF ISBN 978-1-909895-45-4

Printed in Dublin by SPRINT-print Ltd.

In memory of Donal;
dedicated to my family and
all those bereaved by suicide.

Even though I walk through the valley of the shadow
of death, I will fear no evil, for you are with me ...

Psalm 23 (Donal's favourite Psalm)

A.M.D.G.

About the Author

Brendan's love of the outdoors comes from being raised on a farm in Northern Ireland. After studying psychology and information technology at university, he worked in the UK's computer industry as an interface designer. Disillusioned with the 'yuppie' way of life, he resigned to join the Jesuits in Dublin. As a Jesuit student, he worked with young people, leading retreats and pilgrimages. Later, as a priest, he worked with the Gardiner Street Gospel Choir in Dublin and developed his writing skills as editor of the *Irish Jesuit News*. He was school chaplain and photographer in Coláiste Iognáid, Galway before walking the Camino in 2011. A keen hiker, his love of pilgrimage emerged during his Jesuit training when he and a companion begged their way across northern Spain. Brendan is a fluent Spanish speaker from his time studying theology in Colombia. He currently works in spirituality in Belfast.

RedemptionRoadCamino.com

Acknowledgements

I would like to thank my family, including my network of cousins, and all those who helped us grieve the loss of Donal. Special thanks to the Killen family. I'm grateful to the many friends and colleagues who encouraged me on the Camino, those who posted messages on my blog, and especially those who sponsored me to walk for Console, the suicide bereavement charity. I would like to thank in a special way my Jesuit family who supported me all the way; this took the form of much needed accommodation on the Camino in Burgos, Oviedo and Santiago. Particular thanks must go to José de Pablo SJ who was my trip planner and tour guide. Donal Godfrey SJ played a very providential role in Santiago for which I shall be forever grateful.

There were many other nameless people on the Camino who selflessly gave of their time and generosity to help me through. I will never forget the solidarity of the pilgrims I met on the road. Also the volunteers, *hospitaleros*, shopkeepers, bartenders, chemists and many doctors who helped on the Way, and those who just pointed the direction with a smile, not even saying a word.

I am indebted to Pat Coyle, director of Jesuit Communications, who encouraged and helped me with the initial proposal and early stages of writing. Special thanks to Karen Rossignol and Conall O'Cuinn SJ, who reviewed early drafts of the chapters and gave me invaluable feedback and suggestions. My gratitude also goes to Henry Grant SJ, who gave me valuable editorial advice, and Nicole Stapff for her help on translations. Thanks to Paul Kelly and Console who have been there for me and many others at tough moments.

This book was written 'on the move', in a pilgrim fashion, so thanks to the generosity of various Jesuit Communities in Ireland (St Ignatius, Galway; and Peter Faber, Belfast) and Canada (Regis Formation Community, the Jesuit Curia, Toronto; St John's, Newfoundland; and St Ignatius, Guelph (the hermitage)). Thanks to Tony O'Riordan SJ, my constant companion for the original pilgrim insights in 1994's walk. Finally, thanks to Eileen O'Brien and Orpen Press, who have been supportive and skilled, and always encouraged the best writing and production values.

Contents

Foreword

I first met Brendan McManus SJ on a November evening in 2007 when I was sharing my personal story with a Console support group of which he was a member. Having lost my own sister to suicide, I set up the suicide prevention agency Console in 2002 with the desire of supporting others in a similar situation of loss and hopefully prevent others dying in such a tragic way. I was impressed by Brendan's authenticity and particularly his humility in asking for help, a big challenge particularly for grieving males. As a priest Brendan is not afraid to write about his own faith crisis and rage at God, a key theme on this epic journey. Many people will identify with Brendan on the Camino because they will recognise the courageous struggle to keep going, to keep taking the next step and to follow the winding trail wherever it takes you.

Redemption Road tells Brendan's personal story of walking the Camino de Santiago, some 500 miles, in memory of his brother Donal, who had died by suicide. It is a story about fraternal love, but also about loss and the quest for inner peace. The enigmatic trail, the Camino de Santiago in Spain, provides the dramatic backdrop for Brendan's healing quest, with its stunning beauty as well as its enormous physical and personal challenges. As a Jesuit, Brendan uses all the wisdom and tools of the society's founder, Ignatius of Loyola, the quintessential journeyman and saint. His sixteenth-century spirituality, with its pilgrim, decision-based approach, guides Brendan through some difficult situations. He learns how to go at his own pace, to be free of the pressure to compete with others and to 'live in the moment', being present to himself and others.

As the founder of Console, I have a keen interest in how people grieve the death of a loved one, and in this book walking is the therapy that allows Brendan to heal the wounds of the past. This is a story about redemption, about gently mending a broken life through pilgrimage, movement and meditation. The long-distance Camino de Santiago, the medieval pilgrimage route through northern Spain, provides an awesome backdrop of scenery, personalities and culture. Brendan's fluency in Spanish is a crucial entry into this Iberian world. On this trail Brendan experiences a number of adventures and trials which bring his inner tensions to the surface, and paves the way for a deep healing process. Finally, it is a story about spirituality and how it is present in the grit of everyday experience, and about how a sixteenth-century Basque pilgrim, Ignatius of Loyola, illuminates the journey for today.

I was particularly moved when Brendan mentions how important Console was for him and that being part of a support group was an essential part of the healing process. What interests me is the uncovering of successful survival skills or creative ways of coping. Here is a book that does precisely that, in a way that is neither preachy nor prescriptive, but convincing because it is personal. I believe there is something unique about the process of suicide bereavement that literally drives people to the *End of the Earth* (the title of the last chapter) to seek solace for their wounded souls. I found that Brendan's account beautifully describes the human drive for healing, both its difficulties and its consolations, and culminates in an eminently hopeful conclusion.

Paul Kelly
Founder and CEO of Console

Glossary of Spanish Words

albergue or *refugio*	A very basic and cheap hostel designed for Camino walkers
café con leche	Typical sweet Spanish coffee made with milk
Buen Camino	The greeting given to pilgrims: 'Have a great walk'
El Camino	The Way, trail or route; there are many of these pilgrim way-marked routes with yellow arrows, all directing the pilgrims towards Santiago
Camino del Norte	'The Northern Route'; it is the route I walked here, following the coast from the French border before heading inland for Santiago
Camino Francés	The principal Camino route from St-Jean-Pied-de-Port in France, through the Pyrenees and directly west to Santiago
Camino Primitivo	The original Camino route, from Oviedo to Santiago
Compostela	Literally means 'field of stars'; it is the second part of the city's name, Santiago de Compostela, but it is also the name of the certificate given for finishing the Camino
credencial	The special 'pilgrim passport' which has to be stamped wherever you stay and is

	inspected at the end in order to receive the *Compostela*
etapa	A stage or section of the Camino linking hostels, around 20 kilometres long; guidebooks outline one stage per day
flechas amarillas	Yellow arrows that mark the Camino route
hospitalero/a	A volunteer who welcomes pilgrims in certain allied hostels
menu del día	A cheap three-course meal restaurants offer specifically for pilgrims
peregrino	Meaning 'pilgrim'; the one who walks the Camino
posada	Boarding house or small hotel, like a B&B
Santiago	Means 'Saint James'; this city is famous for its cathedral, where St James' remains are reputedly kept, and the destination for all Camino pilgrims
sello	Stamp; each hostel puts a stamp in the pilgrim passport which records the progress of the pilgrims

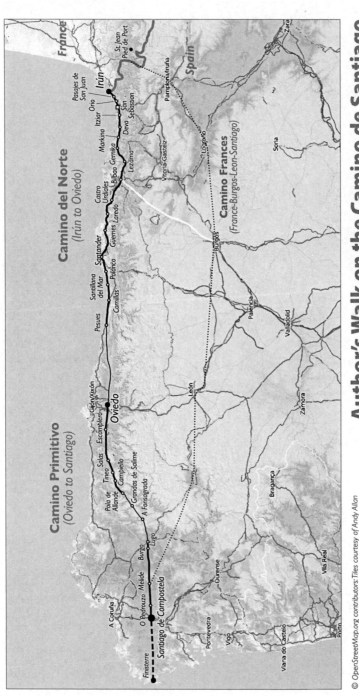

Author's Walk on the Camino de Santiago

Camino del Norte • Camino Primitivo

1

Driven by Desire

Driving rain beat off the retreat house window in Connemara, Galway, as I struggled to lead a group of caged teenagers. The lyrics of Irish band Aslan's song, 'How can I protect you in this crazy world?', rang out on the stereo, Christy Dignam's distinctive vocals finding their mark. The song, intended for their spiritual development, cut through to my inner emptiness and a vague sense of guilt. I turned away so they wouldn't see the pain etched on my face. Despite this, I saw the knowing looks. Irrationally, the song sounded to me as an accusation: how can you believe after tragedy, especially as a Jesuit priest whose job it is to save people? With the arrival of the bus I was relieved to be finished and out of the spotlight. Numb and churned by unexpected grief, I went through the motions in clearing up.

'I can't keep pretending there is not some wound here', I thought to myself on the bus into Galway. Tired of putting on an act, I was fed up feeling out of sorts and scraping by in survival mode. I felt that I was of no use to anyone else unless I made the journey into grief myself. The last few years since my brother Donal's[1] death by suicide had been difficult. Physically, the sickness of the soul revealed itself in terms of shingles, depression and a recurring flu virus. Psychologically, the initial shock, the numbness of the funeral and the aftershock had been devastating, but now there was the low-grade, ongoing silent anguish, not to mention the spiritual crisis that I was only dimly aware of.

As with many other grief survivors, life was a continuous battle: presenting a brave face, while inside everything screamed decay and loss. Many friends, family and colleagues were magnificent in their concern and support, but I needed a little extra help and I hesitantly consulted counsellors and other healing professions. Eventually, I found Console, a suicide support group; it was a safe place to be myself, express my feelings and share with peers who had lived through the same horror. Still there was something left unhealed; how could I trust in life again and transform this experience of loss into new life and outreach? As a priest with a faith crisis I was living a contradiction, communicating a loving God was challenging. Life had changed dramatically; with suicide the veil had been lifted and there was no going back to old sureties. I couldn't keep limping along like this for much longer; something radical was required to reawaken my passion and energy.

On that bus journey, the story of the forced convalescence of St Ignatius of Loyola sprang to my mind. A Basque courtier who became founder of the Jesuits (my order), he lived almost 500 years ago. A prototypical psychologist, he began examining his inner moods and feelings. A cannonball had shattered his leg and forced him to spend months in bed reflecting and fantasizing. This experience and a subsequent walking pilgrimage were the catalysts for a radical process of transformation. Significantly, the isolation of his sickbed meant he had to forgo his favourite romantic novels, which were unavailable, for a *Life of Christ* and of the saints. He still fantasized about his romantic aspirations however, and alternated these with the more spiritual reading, using his imagination to picture radically different scenarios. In one daydream he would win the hand of a famous lady, while in another he would outdo the saints in fasts and pilgrimages. He made a strange discovery on his couch, that while:

> ... thinking of worldly matters he found much delight, but after growing weary and dismissing them he found that he was *dry and unhappy*. But when he thought of imitating the saints, he not only found consolation but even afterwards he remained *happy and joyful*.[2]

The contrasting moods that resulted were deeply significant. He deduced that God was communicating directly with him, inviting him to reflect and make decisions, ultimately leading him to a profoundly different life.[3] The heart of his insight was that his superficial desires (self-serving) were not genuinely life-giving and resulted in unhappy, desolating feelings. However, his deepest desires (serving others) were by contrast invigorating and rewarding and resulted in happy and consoling feelings. Illness forced him outwards into the joyful challenge of life over half-living in a comfortable desolation.

Though I knew this story well, what struck me was the way his illness became a crucible for transformation. My own illness and resultant moods seemed to find an echo in Ignatius' experience; the answers could be found through pilgrimage, self-awareness and reflection.[4] Similarly, I had to choose between different life-giving or deadening alternatives, and this choice led irrevocably to action, a journey or a quest. As soon as he was well, Ignatius the pilgrim limped his way to Jerusalem and into a new life. Ignatius formulated all his experiential wisdom on moods and decisions into a spiritual manual called the Spiritual Exercises,[5] a guide I use extensively. Ignatius had known great depression and desolation, and lived through his own 'dark night'. He had even contemplated suicide once. My own story and desire seemed to find a striking parallel in Ignatius.

I had a vivid memory of a 30-day pilgrimage that I had done as part of my Jesuit training some 20 years previously in Spain, walking in the actual footsteps of Ignatius, begging for food and lodging.[6] This was one of the defining moments of my vocation, where paradoxically I had felt free even though I had nothing, full even though I was hungry, and alive even though living a precarious existence. My intuition told me I needed to get back to that primitive aloneness with God of being on the road, radically open to life. Having tasted that once, I desired that again. At the age of 50 I knew that I couldn't go begging; however, I could still hike and carry a backpack.

An aficionado of pilgrimages, I was intrigued by the legendary Camino de Santiago and had read extensively on it. I had seen the movie *The Way*,[7] with Martin Sheen, which movingly dealt with grief and loss through walking. The seeds of an idea began germinating in my head: I could walk the ancient route to Santiago, searching to recover the 'lost passion'[8] and put together the fragments of my life. I welcomed the necessary asceticism, the abandoning of myself to the vagaries of the road, and the creation of silence through the meditative rhythm of walking.

I wanted to listen to my heart, to be in contact with nature, and to live from the deepest part of myself, like Ignatius. I would bring a symbol of my brother to Santiago on behalf of my family. Merely saying the words in conversation, 'to walk the Camino', produced a visceral change in me, igniting a fire. I took it as confirmation that this was a genuine desire[9] in me and that somehow my healing was tied to it. The Camino wasn't just a trip or a stroll but a search for spiritual survival, reshaping the broken pieces in some meaningful way. A journey into the unknown, it was simultaneously thrilling and terrifying.

That winter I set about planning the trip, exploring guidebooks, websites and blogs. I gathered particular hiking equipment and began planning for this 800 kilometre walk.

There was a glut of information and advice on the Camino, not all of it coherent. For example, it was confusing that there is no fixed starting point but only one destination; there is a 'pilgrim passport' but no borders. There are in fact multiple Caminos to Santiago, not just one. There are as many opinions on walking the Camino as there are people, and widely different motivations or philosophies for walking this ancient road.

After much reflection, I decided to walk the Camino de Santiago in this manner:

- I would walk alone as a pilgrim;[10] this was a solo quest and I wanted time to sort out my head, reflect and meditate.
- I would walk the much less travelled northern route, *Camino del Norte* (not the classic *Camino Francés*), 800 kilometres west along the coast from the French border; though short on infrastructure it was much more scenic.
- As a symbol I would bring Donal's old Barcelona FC T-shirt to place on the altar in Santiago on behalf of my family.
- I would collect sponsorship for the Console suicide prevention organisation in Ireland which I had been involved with.
- My inspiration and guide would be St Ignatius of Loyola, the walker and pilgrim,[11] using his Spiritual Exercises to guide me.

Normally a weekend hiker, I had to do extra training before departing, walking mountains around the west of Ireland with a pack full of bricks. Packing the night before departure was a frantic back and forth on the bathroom scales to reduce weight. A drizzly morning in early June saw me on the tarmac at Dublin Airport, my cape pulled around me. Waiting on the plane steps I shivered in my light hiking clothes, anticipating Spain's warmer climes. My backpack weighed in at 7.7 kg on the check-in scales, the result of ruthless repacking that meant abandoning my sleeping bag.[12] Still tired from my job, I slept all the way on the plane and suddenly was melting in the 25-degree heat of Biarritz, France.

Waiting for the train to Irún, my starting point on the French–Spanish border, I fell in with a seasoned Canadian pilgrim, Jim, doing the French route for the tenth time. Though strangers, we quickly became friends united by our hiking gear and common destination, my first experience of the unique Camino bond. We exchanged stories of what drew us to the Camino. Even though he had more experience, I was immediately struck by his humility, radiating peace and a willingness to offer advice. We took off in opposite directions; he was for Saint-Jean-Pied-de-Port. I was never to see him again.

As I boarded the local train alone, I felt a mix of excitement and anxiety, imagining myself on the mythical Camino de Santiago the next day. The train jolted to a stop in the French border town of Hendaye, where it awaited a connection. I realised that I could save an hour by simply walking 3 kilometres into Irún in Spain. Slowly and deliberately I hoisted my Camino backpack for the first time and strolled up a very nondescript street into Spain's Basque Country. At the border, I paused at the International Bridge of Santiago, a fitting start for my pilgrimage. I made a heartfelt prayer, asking for protection, courage and health for the next month. It was an anticlimactic start to the Camino. I had anticipated in my mind a huge gateway, a crowd of locals, a dramatic feeling; there was nothing but a tar road, rusting bridge and distant terracotta roofs.

The two towns were so intertwined I was in Irún before I knew it. I approached my first church on the Camino, the imposing seventeenth-century Santa Maria de Juncal. Expecting medieval-style hospitality, I was met with locked doors. Somewhat put out, I composed my pilgrim prayer on the doorstep. Then there was nothing for it but to find the *albergue* (a very basic and cheap hostel designed for Camino walkers), which was a cramped double apartment by the railway. It had been some years since I slept in a bunk so imagine my horror when I realised that there was no door on the rooms and I would be effectively sharing with all 30 occupants. The hostel owner sensed my discomfort, my squeaky new clothes revealing a greenhorn, and drew me in with a smile. He was extremely helpful in indicating the next day's walk, called an *etapa* or stage, and indicated on the map where to stay. He gave me my first official stamp (*sello*) in my *credencial* (pilgrim's passport, which is stamped everywhere you stay and inspected at the end to get the *Compostela*, the certificate given for finishing the Camino), which was strangely reassuring given that this was the beginning of something largely unknown as yet.

I regretted leaving the sleeping bag as I hardly slept with the cold. It was not a good start for a 30-day walking marathon. Getting up at 6.30 a.m. was a shock to the system and it took me about 40 sluggish minutes to get my gear sorted. Once outside, a dappled sunrise dispelled my fears and, feeling expansive, I took a side trip to Hondarribia to see and taste the ocean. Talking to some locals I knew I was in Basque territory, with its unique colours, spirit and language. There on the quayside was the dramatic start to the Camino I sought – a huge poem displayed in Basque and Spanish that began:

> The Camino invites, you discover; you can take a detour from it anytime you want. It is a way of water and earth that you cross by bridge or boat; it takes you away from the sound of traffic and brings you to the murmur of the river, to the ceaseless movement of tides charged with salty air.[13]

It was a curious, contemplative take on the Camino, yet food for my pilgrim soul.

Unfortunately, I wasn't prepared for the huge hill I encountered rejoining the trail at Guadalupe Sanctuary. Any vestiges of poetry or mystique were soon dispelled perspiring along a busy winding road, with the clatter of construction up ahead. I paused a moment to light a candle in the charming chapel at Guadalupe. After a paltry lunch in the car park, as I had forgotten to get provisions, I continued along a charming hillside trail. Its scrub bushes and deep red soil reminded me of hill walks around Dublin. The rest of the afternoon seemed effortless though the trail was dusty. I was enchanted with the tinkling of cowbells and sharp tang of goats. It augured well for the Camino, if only I could keep grounded in 'one step at a time', and walk day by day.

I finally arrived in Pasajes de San Juan, a lovely little traditional fishing port cut out of sandstone cliffs. Famished, I had tuna casserole in a café for dinner and then strolled along the dramatic cliff path above a turquoise sea. Eventually, I found a sheltered wildflower garden for a siesta while waiting for the hostel to open. On first sight the Hospital de Peregrinos was bright and welcoming. The *hospitalero* (hostel manager), Felice, was the perfect host, going to great lengths to make me feel welcome. My bunk was in a spacious and airy loft with only three others – sheer luxury.

Felice took me aside conspiratorially and told me there was one crucial thing about the Camino. It was the first real test of my rusty Spanish. I wondered what he was building up to – some personal safety warning maybe or certain places to avoid. With much gravitas he announced, 'To avoid getting lost on the Camino always follow the *flechas amarillas* [yellow arrows].' He explained to me: 'there are different systems of marking the Way[14] in different regions of northern Spain – shells, arrow posts – but they can mean different things depending on the region. The hand-painted yellow arrows however, will always point you in the right direction. They will appear every 200 metres or so; all you have to do is be alert to them.' In fact, it was to prove one of the most useful pieces of advice I received and saved me a lot of wasted time. Felice (sounding like the Spanish word for happy, *feliz*) was well named.

Happy that I had not overexerted myself on my first real day of walking, I took a leisurely stroll along the harbour as the sun melted into the sea. Just opposite, I could see the next day's walk, which was an almost vertical ascent up the craggy hillside. Having gone hungry that day, I remembered to buy ample provisions for the following day's lunch. In the plaza I met two women walkers, one Italian and one Dutch, and we chatted warmly over a drink and some clam chowder. It wasn't long until we got down to business – why we were walking the Camino. This is a common topic among hikers. Protective of my own privacy, I was somewhat vague ('midlife crisis'), but that question was to echo more and more in me. Well tired at this stage, I slept in a dreamless bliss, snug under a hostel blanket.

The next day was over before I knew it. Footsore and tired, I limped into Orio in the late afternoon in the company of two Spanish men I had met on the way. I noticed a rhythm developing even at this early stage: a 6 a.m. start, walk all morning, make your own lunch, find an *albergue* before it gets hot, a pilgrim Mass in town, and a long afternoon spent reading or reflecting before a cheap *menu del día* meal. The private hostel in Orio was something special, even if it was a bit dearer (€10) than the municipal ones. In the basement of a family home, it was clean and bright with extensive views of endless interlocking green hills.

I was coming to know the ecstasies and agonies of the famed *Camino del Norte*, however. The steep hills were tough on a hiker, requiring considerable toil and sweat. I already scaled two substantial mountains in a day of ascending and descending. I had seen the glorious city of San Sebastian and its crescent beaches. It was surreal trekking along the immaculate, deserted city promenades first thing in the morning, trying to find the quirky yellow arrows. However, the real payoff was the views – the sea always in sight with its soaring cliffs and rising gulls. The places were all distinctly Basque: the cryptic road signs, people's speech and the architecture.

Orio had some lovely sixteenth-century houses with intricate carvings on their sandstone lintels.

Even though I was only three days into the journey, it felt like an eternity, as if I had entered another dimension where time had slowed and life was different. More and more I savoured the morning walks, a meditative invitation to get into a stride and surrender to it. I had not experienced any great insight yet, simply operating on a survival level: eating, walking, drinking, talking and sleeping. Doing my Review of the Day[15] that night, I was surprised to find that I had been in a positive, upbeat mood all day. Ignatius named this 'consolation' and it seemed to confirm my deep desire to be on the Way.

2

An Inner Light

It was wondrous being on the go as the dawn arrived, a golden, ethereal light. I watched it inhabit the outside landscape, virtually bringing it into being. It evoked an essential reverence as I took to the road. The thrill of anticipating the day ahead overshadowed the corporeal struggle to get moving. Bleary eyed and muscle stiff, I soon thawed in the sun's warmth on the main street. In response to nature's light display an inner glow was kindled in me.

I scuttled across the deserted town's quays, over the River Oria, and into the welcoming woods. The inviting trail was a gravel path that wound its way under the highway and up the hill. I eased into the walking rhythm in the cool morning air, the only sound the click of the walking poles. Happiness overtook me like a lost friend; I couldn't believe I was fit, healthy and like a medieval pilgrim on a sacred quest to St James' tomb. Everything seemed possible and optimism surged with every step. Santiago seemed like just a few easy days' walk away.

I was thinking about my brother Donal in the halcyon days before 'the great sadness'. He had been this little cheeky blond-haired tyke always getting into trouble. Football mad, he would play for hours at a neighbour's house, his passion and commitment evident even then. He was smart and witty as a teenager, and his sense of humour and big broad grin charmed all around him. With a natural ability for analysis and strategy, he excelled at bridge, even winning a congress with our father while still a youth. His football exploits saw him play for his club and even as a county minor at Croke Park's hallowed turf in Dublin. He later worked in farming and construction, but very few knew that he had a PhD from the University of Ulster. Probably his greatest gift was his compassion for others: he gave almost all of his money to charity, and he would go to extraordinary lengths to help someone in trouble. One story had him use the curtains from one of his rental apartments to cover a friend who was homeless. This was a talented, outgoing, sporty man who had a big heart; he was the light of our lives. This was my brother Donal.

Climbing higher into the hills near Zarautz, the forest cleared and I entered a wine region. The bright green vines stood out against the dark forest and red soil. Arranged in rows, it was all very ordered and cultivated. I met a man coming out of a vineyard and we fell into conversation. His leathery skin betrayed much time spent outdoors and he carried an old pair of pruning shears. He told me he was busy trimming the vines that surrounded his property in order to keep them productive.[16] It reminded me of the penitential aspects of the Camino, the necessary asceticism that is an inevitable part of any courageous endeavour.[17] Living simply and without luxury focuses the mind on deeper values and longer-term spiritual rewards. I could see some benefits in interior freedom, humility and awareness already. Peering closely at some vines, I could distinguish how pruned bushes were much more productive. I didn't realise how apt this metaphor would be later in the journey.

A descending trail of switchbacks brought me to the sea again at Zarautz. I took some time out on the wonderful promenade to contemplate the waves. Stopping at a local coffee shop for breakfast, the *café con leche* (coffee made with milk) was blissfully sweet and the croissants filling after a two-hour fast. The sun beamed in through the tinted window and I felt pleasantly warm and drowsy. Reluctantly, I gathered my gear together and asked the way to the Camino. To my surprise the entire café, with typical Latin enthusiasm, all gave me directions simultaneously and by different routes.

I was shortly back up in the mountains again, surrounded by butterflies and lost in the Zen of walking.[18] I traversed roads, forests and fields in an ever-changing pastoral landscape. At a mountain crossroads I met an older man with a tracheotomy tube in his neck and, though he had difficulty speaking, he very kindly briefed me on the trail ahead. He was at pains to point out the local hermitage that had been damaged by recent road works. This was walking heaven however: the jewel of the Basque Country with endless farmland framed by forest. At one stage I lay down in an idyllic wildflower meadow for a siesta but unfortunately woke up covered in bites. Translucent butterflies still surrounded me however.

As I came out of the forest onto a remote paved road, I mistook a house bedecked with soft drink advertising for a café. Out of water and parched, I knocked urgently on the door and was taken aback to find out it was a private house. Laughing at my mistake, the owners graciously filled my water bottle and invited me in. When they learned that I was Irish, they insisted that their teenage daughter practice her English with me. I could sense the pride of the parents as we conversed briefly. It was a moment I wanted to hold onto forever: a simple human exchange, but significant in that it was pregnant with the hopes and dreams of this Basque family. I was humbled.

Looking at the map I was thrilled to see that I was only 15 kilometres from the birthplace of my Basque guide and inspiration, Ignatius of Loyola. A huge basilica and Jesuit residence now encompass his family home, the iconic Castle of Loyola.[19] In 1521, during his convalescence experience here, he first woke up to the significance of inner moods and discernment.[20] He subsequently wrote the Spiritual Exercises as a guidebook for trainers helping others to have the same enlightenment. The Exercises use the analogy of physical exercise, which is useful for getting in shape, fighting flab and maintaining health, and applies it to spiritual practices that promote integration, freedom and healing.[21] This often implies renewal or restoration: bringing light into the darkness of our lives, healing wounds and destructive tendencies.[22] I could relate it to the darkness of my grief experience and the hope of rekindling the inner flame. Likewise Donal, originally a person of light, had been overtaken by the darkness of depression and suicide. Now, in death, I believed that the divine light would eclipse whatever shadow or negativity he suffered; he would be restored by God.[23] The Camino was a 'spiritual exercise' therefore, a pilgrimage offered for the good of his soul, I thought, not realising what was in store for me. Redemption, being restored or healed, was the goal. The Camino provided the ideal way to achieve this: shedding the darkness of unhelpful attachments,[24] and glimpsing the light of transformation.

The shadows were long when I got into Itziar after 28 kilometres, the furthest I had walked. The heat was fierce in the last climb up to the village and my legs were spent. Sore and sunburnt, I was dehydrated and out of energy. I was dismayed to find that there was no hostel in the village, and the 6 kilometres to the next one felt impossible. It was then I understood the wisdom of planning the walk in stages (*etapas*) so that the hostels are a walkable distance from each other. My guidebook listed a nearby rural hostel that ran a shuttle service and some kind Spanish pilgrims rang to book a place on my behalf. After an hour's wait, I discovered that the owner would only collect groups, and so I was stranded. With night approaching I also turned down a lift to the next town, as I didn't want to skip a section (how ironic this would be later). Thoroughly beaten, I collapsed into a cheap hotel and an early night. When I reflected back on the day however, it had been rewarding. The beauty of nature and the kindness of strangers predominated. My enduring image was of the pervasive butterflies and their whimsical flight.

Next morning I woke up the worst for wear, feeling my age and the sting of lactic acid in my muscles. I could hardly get out of bed and the euphoria of the previous day rapidly dissipated. Feeling I had overstretched myself, I resolved to be more moderate in my planning. Breakfast in the tiny hotel was simple but tasty. I still felt a bit foolish for not making it to a hostel, but I was philosophical about it as I was still learning the ropes. Determined to walk within my own limits, I resolved not to be dictated to by the guidebook, other walkers or circumstances.[25] Too much of my life had been spent ignoring my body and my instincts and I had paid the price. I had an extra week in hand, just in case I needed more time. Backpack on, I stepped outside from the tranquil comfort into a flurry of wind and rain. How could two days be so different, and how could I feel so reluctant and fatigued now?

The first time I saw Adrian walking toward me he looked like he had been through the wars, with his trousers muddied to the knees and his cape flying in the wind. He was thin and wiry, just over 60 years old, very focused and determined. We fell in together and initially it was a struggle to understand each other. I learned that he was Dutch, retired and also walking alone. He couldn't believe that I was only getting starting in mid-morning and that I was taking it easy. My explanation that I had made a mistake with the stages and had to get in sync didn't seem to impress him. We stopped to take off our rain gear but soon the rain restarted. As we were going down a very steep concrete lane greasy with run-off, he started to slip and the next thing I knew my feet were going from under me too. We ended up walking on the narrow grass verge for safety, relishing our shrewd escape. It started to rain again and out came the waterproof gear; it was a tedious process that we were to repeat often. Within an hour we arrived in the quirky town of Deva,[26] our destination.

We had to take a special elevator down the hillside to the town centre as it was so steep. In the elevator we met two locals who insisted on bringing us to the tourist office. After the all-important stamp in our *credenciales*, they gave us a key to get into the hostel that was located back up on the hill. Walking back, Adrian was delighted to get into the hostel so early, saying, 'You are my good luck for today; five minutes ago we didn't have anything and now all this.' Then he said an even stranger thing: 'That is what it is like every day on the Camino, good things just happen.' It struck me as true to my own limited experience so far, that when you are open and free all manner of good things follow. I stored these words carefully in my brain.

The hostel was an old abandoned sports centre that smelled of damp and accumulated sweat. Once set up in the hostel, I went for a swim[27] at Lapari beach, a deserted sandy cove at the mouth of the harbour. In an adventurous mood, I had a look around town, beginning with the sea cliffs and the busy port. I was drawn to the town jewel, the church of Santa María la Real, with its Gothic entrance and fortified facade. Though built in the fifteenth and sixteenth centuries (the time of Ignatius), it was the seventeenth-century baroque altarpiece that drew me to Mass there. Not an expert in church architecture, I have nevertheless been fascinated by how a building reflects the spirit and faith of the time. Designed as a place of encounter between the divine and the human, this largely renaissance space was about order, light and symmetry. Looking up, I marvelled at the ribbed vault, a triumph of uncluttered order. I was reflecting on Ignatius' idea of balance,[28] an ordered life that frees us to be our true selves: a light for the world.[29] I had a quiet afternoon wandering around a sleepy town. My only purchase was a new penknife as I had lost my old one.

Back in the hostel I had time to reflect on the phenomenon of the Camino after some hard-earned experience. It was a cross between extreme hiking, ascending some 500 metres of altitude every day carrying a backpack, and hostelling, which meant sharing an international communal space for laundry, dinner and socialising. The beaches and the high passes were magnificent of course, but you could be forgiven for wondering who designed such a testing route. Without doubt my favourite part of the daily routine was getting up early, slipping silently out of the hostel, and ambling up a deserted country trail. After that, just simply 'follow the yellow arrows' as my host Felice in San Juan had said.

The simplicity of life became beguiling, doing ordinary things (eating, sleeping, walking, praying) but with great awareness and presence. The mere motion of walking through Basque valleys and meadows was transformed into prayer or contemplation, realising that I was a creature searching for the creator. Just as contemplation is a wordless communication with the divine, walking facilitates this process of inner silence and wordless intimacy. I knew well the trap of being stuck 'in the head' and falling prey to guilt, remorse and rumination. Having lived in the shadow of grief and desolation too long, I desperately craved some spiritual renovation. I felt that Ignatius, the archetypal contemplative and pilgrim, would have approved of this freedom quest.[30]

The next day I was first up and left the hostel in the dark; my legs felt good and I felt the benefit of sleep and rest. The guidebook[31] described the forthcoming day's walk thus:

> This is a beautiful but difficult high level route through some very remote country. It would be unwise to tackle this in bad weather if you were alone or unsure of your capabilities.

I reckon I ticked both of those boxes right off. Fortunately, the weather was good and made the going much easier. The morning light shimmered in the trees and the mist slowly burned off the peaks. The dirt track seemed to wind endlessly up through pine forests and valleys. Early in the day I caught up with a limping Austrian man but he rejected all attempts at conversation. I was to meet him several times that day but he never returned a greeting. Coming to understand the need for silence and radical aloneness, I finally let him be. Alone again, I was wrapped in the stillness of a pine forest for the morning and then, later, a scented eucalyptus one. It was an ecstasy of rural solitude.

Later, I fell in with a group of Italians and one Spaniard, with whom I could communicate. I was very glad of their company at that stage as I was starting to flag, and my right foot was sore. It was getting hot now and the last downhill section was particularly difficult. I felt like I was being carried by the group and even though little was said, there was an unspoken camaraderie. We arrived in Markina around 1 p.m. and though I had intended to walk on to the next village where the hostel was a monastery, I thought the better of it. I was fairly done in and glad to sit around with the others outside a bar. Adrian was among the group; even though we had not seen each other all day or spoken a word, there was this understanding between us.

The hostel was at the rear of a church and there was quite a crowd of pilgrims waiting. The volunteer *hospitaleros* arrived late, a real test for all of us who were hot, sweaty and hungry. It was frustrating waiting for the hostel to open, but cultivating patience was my only option. I had an interesting conversation with an older Spaniard who was doing the route in a camper van. Living the Camino ideal, he lamented the state of the world and the damage caused by individualism and consumerism. He contrasted this with the Camino where there is so much time to be with yourself and to be conscious of others and the world around you. I knew what he was talking about, on the Way you are outside time, looking in on the world and its crazy ways.

Down to the Bone

Unable to sleep, I went down to the front door where there was a small group smoking and relaxing. I quickly realised these were *hospitaleros*, the volunteers who ran the *albergue*. I heard them say they were from Barcelona, and just for fun I said that I was from there too. This livened up things somewhat and brought me a lot of teasing. This is exactly what Donal would have done, I thought, using humour to help break barriers. When the jokes ran out we moved on to more serious matters, talking about neuro-linguistic programming[32] and other therapies. To my surprise, one of the women admitted that she needed urgent help with depression and anxiety. A number of others interjected, trying to calm her, but she shrugged them off. She then zeroed in on me, asking me for specific advice. This was particularly distressing given Donal's history. I repeated the advice I had given him: 'Get good help, get the best professional help and get it fast.' Excusing myself, I left to go to bed. Afterwards in my bunk, I found it hard to let go of the woman's dilemma. How had this same issue followed me here to a remote corner of Spain? What did it mean? One thing was certain: the Camino was already challenging me deeply on how free I was of the past. Was this part of a process of stripping away all pretence and having the real me emerge? It was too early to say.

I remembered a morning over 20 years earlier, driving Donal to see a specialist in mood disorders. Very worried, I had taken time off work to try to support my brother. Getting help for him was nerve-wracking as it was unfamiliar territory and carried some stigma. It was difficult to hand intimate health secrets over to a virtual stranger, not knowing if it would improve things. We met with the doctor and he prescribed some medication but Donal only temporarily adhered to the regime. In subsequent years he went through the same cycle: getting advice, ignoring it and getting worse. I could only look on in dismay. He got progressively worse and the symptoms were more sharply defined, even though he showed none of this to the world. I could feel him slipping away and, like the rest of my family, I was powerless to help.

As time went on Donal became more unreachable, my worry intensified and my attempts to reach him became more futile. As someone whose job it was to help people, it was particularly excruciating to be subjected to a slow, protracted freeze out and to watch someone I loved disintegrate before my eyes. While much of this was attributable to depression, it was hard not to take it personally or feel some guilt. Loaded with haunting memories, I was distressed to be asked that same question on help for depression. Having learned through bitter experience that I couldn't save anyone however, I knew that the *hospitalera* had to make her own choice to seek help. I went to sleep.

I left the hostel the next morning in a sombre mood, a grey dawn creeping over the Basque countryside. After over an hour of hard walking, however, I realised that I had left my walking poles back at the hostel. After a moment of frustration, I weighed up whether or not to go back and finally decided to walk on, feeling more like a simple pilgrim. Did I really need them after all?

To make matters worse, I lost my way in the hills for over two hours. I had faithfully followed the yellow arrows up a steep hill and through a small mountain village. Some indistinct arrows took me into an alpine meadow, I must have missed a turn, and I had difficulty following an increasingly faint track. Suddenly I came onto a sheer face, surrounded by pine trees. I could see my destination on the next hill dead ahead, and the urge was to go straight there, but there was no way forward. I called out for help several times; no answer. I had to resist the destructive urge to keep pushing forward; rather this was a time for careful discernment. Ignatius of Loyola is identified with good decision making, but even he had to learn through reflection on bitter experience.[33] His main insight for a good decision was to become free from any undue influence, poised like the midpoint of a balance.[34] Uncovering the biases or sometimes hidden influences was the real challenge for him as it was for me.

Examining my present situation, I realised I was driven by an irrational desire to find a way against all odds, vainly trying to control an escalating situation to find a shortcut, at all costs. This approach of making impulsive decisions was putting me in some danger. I had to let go of my pride and eat humble pie, admitting I was lost and turning around. The most difficult thing was letting go of control,[35] accepting that the Camino was bigger than I was, and that I needed help and guidance to help me stay on track. Poignantly, this had been Donal's downfall. It was my introduction to a great insight: *you don't walk the Camino, it walks you.*

Eventually, I retraced my steps to the village nearby. A local directed me back down the hill to Bolivar village where, frustratingly, I had just come from. At this stage I could actually see the monastery where I was headed but I would have to take a winding detour to get there. Those costly extra kilometres gave me space for reflection on detours, detachment and what might have happened. Fortunately, I was back on track shortly without a scratch, but with a new attitude and respect for the arrows and guidebook.

In the afternoon I fell into step with my Dutch friend, Adrian, whom I hadn't walked with for two days. Amazingly, I discovered he was 75 years old and fit as a fiddle. Not having any common language, we merely walked in silence, which suited us both. As we started up a huge hill covered in pine trees, I began to flag but Adrian showed no signs of slowing down. I was glad of the company, even as I trailed in his wake. We approached a farmyard and, out of habit, I picked a stick up from a hedge. There was an exceedingly nasty-looking black dog tied up on a chain, snarling at us. Suddenly, he came loose, making a beeline for us with feral ferocity. Adrian came in behind me and I beat the stick on the ground, holding him off with the point of it. In a bizarre waltz, we worked our way through the farmyard and retreated from the dog, which was now in a virtual frenzy. The owner appeared and I shouted at him that the dog was free. Unfazed by the attack on us, he nonchalantly tied up the dog again to our great relief. It was another narrow escape in what was a stressful day. On the outskirts of Gernika, I ran out of water and had to ask a local woman for assistance. Finding the *albergue* was easy and, after a quick meal, I took an early night.

The next morning was a slow start. Though it was still early as I walked the largely deserted streets out of Gernika, here and there a few bakeries and coffee shops were springing to life. I noticed a few young people unsteady on their feet, obviously on their way home from the night before. I asked one young man for directions and, reeking of liquor, he insisted on guiding me. He asked me where I was from; upon hearing me say Northern Ireland, he went off on a tirade about the IRA and the 'struggle for independence'. He went on to tell me about the Basque fight for independence, and how disappointed he was at the lack of results. He impressed on me the urgency of the struggle as he guided me onwards, getting more animated and drawing me into a close camaraderie. My last memory of him was of him punching his fist in the air; I couldn't resist calling out *'Vive la república!'* to him as we parted.

I began a steep ascent almost immediately, and shortly I was back up in the mountains again, alone on a high ridge. The rising sun slowly evaporated the mist lingering in the contours of the valleys. I was witnessing something transient but precious, the normally unseen transition to day. It touched me deeply and tears welled up as I walked this pathway swathed in such beauty. Solitude here did not mean loneliness. Eventually I stopped for a rest at one of the many local houses that offered pilgrims water. I was heartened to see the group of Italians whom I had met a few days ago, now my friends. There were maybe twelve or so of us walkers spread out over the *etapa* on a given day and we would all meet at night. I stopped in a sleepy little village for the ubiquitous *café con leche*. The last part of the afternoon was tough, as unusually the Camino followed a main road, a sign we were getting close to Bilbao. It made for fast walking but it wasn't very pleasant as there was no scenic view and the roar of cars dispelled any contemplative urge.

As I came to the town of Lezama, a well-dressed woman strode intently up the street for what I guessed was a church service. I followed her for about a kilometre until we came upon the reddish stone church of Santa María with an extensive veranda. I met some very friendly people on the way in, who were very interested to know who I was and where I had come from. The Catholic Mass was in Basque, which made it was impossible to understand, but there was a unmistakable strong community presence. My eyes focused on the striking baroque altarpiece in front of me. The red sandstone walls helped to create a subtle glow in the nave that warmed the heart. Praying alone afterwards, I felt some solace and warmth, and asked for help with this walk as it seemed to be getting more difficult and beyond my abilities.[36]

As if in answer to my prayer, a woman came up and introduced herself; she was the local *albergue* coordinator (*hospitalera*) and she invited me to accompany her to the hostel. I took it as a sign that my day's walking was over and was relieved at her kindness. She embodied hospitality in her enthusiasm and knowledge, and filled me in on the local services for pilgrims. She brought me to the hostel and I showered and changed – a small rejuvenating luxury. As she had to go off for a while, she asked me to look after the hostel. I was in my element with my new-found authority, booking people in and telling them where to place their bags. That evening at our pilgrim meal I realised we were becoming a small community: the Italians; my friend Adrian; Anuk, a Dutch woman in between jobs; a Belgian dad getting away from it all; and a Spanish translator. We were bound by our common journey, our unique stories and our flesh and blood humanity revealed by the road. Treasuring this moment and yet conscious of the constant challenge, the levels of providence and exposure on the Camino demanded great flexibility.

The next morning I couldn't believe my luck when I spotted a walking pole left behind in the recycling bin. Though there was only a single ski pole it cheered me up enormously. I also picked up an old pair of hiking socks; I had been having trouble with my right foot and was convinced that these thicker socks would sort that out. Re-equipped and renovated, I strode out of Lezama feeling great. Bilbao was 10 kilometres away and only a small hill lay in my path. On the ascent my left leg started to act up – a niggling pain at first and then a throbbing ache that I couldn't walk off. It was aggravated by the uphill climb; I had no choice but to turn back.

The toughest thing was passing my companions going the opposite way and having to wish them '*Buen Camino*'.[37] Hobbling off the hill and having to seek medical help was a bitter pill to swallow. Fortunately I was only 1 kilometre from the town of Zamudio, which was on the local rail network for

Bilbao. While waiting, I noticed a pharmacy just outside the station. The chemist went to great lengths to help me with my sore leg, getting me the right creams and tablets, though he also advised me to check it out with a doctor. He insisted I take some blister pads and foot cream, at no charge. Glumly riding the train into town, I strained to see my friends on the brown hills. I wondered if they were okay, especially if they were hydrated as the sun was beating down.

At this stage my foot was really hurting and I thought I would not be able to walk much further. I limped my way to a suburb called Portugalete, which I thought would have plenty of services. I found the tourist office to ask for a *pensión* (cheap hotel) and directions for medical help. To my great relief, the man in the tourist office was exceptionally helpful. He got me all the maps, the addresses of the *pensiónes*, and even located the local hospital for me. As it was late I would have to go the next day, so I basked outside in the sun by the river having a chorizo, cheese and salad baguette. I was grateful for him and all the good people I had met on this walk. Afterwards, I checked into a slightly seedy *pensión* overlooking the Nervion River. The shower didn't work but I figured that you can't have everything. The staff, fortunately, were exceedingly friendly.

The next morning, I tried not to think about my companions trekking ahead of me on the next *etapa*. I was barely able to walk, and I dreaded finding out what was wrong. After breakfast I limped[38] up the hill to the hospital, anxious for some expert advice to resolve the issue. On a particularly steep street of Portugalete I asked directions from a woman selling lottery tickets. She casually suggested a health centre directly behind her instead, saying it would save me time and effort. Intrigued, I went in and had to wait a few minutes to get processed. After fifteen minutes, I was seen by a friendly but efficient doctor. She had me diagnosed and dispatched in ten minutes but it was not good news. She explained it as *estrés tibial anterior*: inflammation of the muscle causing pain in the shin bone (tibia), basically a shin splint. I could be out for a few weeks with this, in which case it would be game over. Or I could try resting it, rubbing in a special cream and taking anti-inflammatories for the pain. I would know the outcome in a few days.

A mixture of emotions, I walked gingerly down the hill to my friendly *pensión*. The owner was very sympathetic and inquired after my diagnosis and treatment. The ignominy of having to return home early tore into my consciousness; how would I face family and friends who had sponsored me? Faced with the prospect of sitting around aimlessly for several days, I knew I had to get away. I called my friend José de Pablo, a Jesuit who lived in Burgos, some 120 kilometres away. It would be a break from the Camino but I could still return and resume where I left off. On calling him, José kindly dropped everything and drove to Bilbao to pick me up.

Packing in the fading luxury of the *pensión*, I was in low mood, thinking that this might be the end of my Camino. My injury put the whole experience into sharp focus for me, now that it might be ending. There was something powerfully compelling, almost addictive, about walking the Camino. It was tough, physically and mentally, and there were few luxuries, but it was profoundly rewarding. The payoff was the elusive 'being in the moment' awareness that it brought and the falling away of other concerns. There was a real connection – with others, oneself and the world. There was something real and embodied about Camino life, as close and personal as breathing, but at the same time transcendent and sacred. Simple memories, such as tying my shoes, swinging my rucksack on my back and breathing deeply when faced with the Iberian unknown, had been utterly thrilling.

The Camino always challenged me: what would happen that day? Who would I meet? Would I find openness in me and the other? The question was, will I find life and consolation? For Ignatius it was about sensitivity to the divine speaking in and through the ordinary events of the day.[39]

Being a pilgrim strips away protective insulation and accentuates the sense of trusting dependency, stepping out into the unknown. Every day is an act of trust, confident that all will be resolved on the road. However, this reminiscing was making me forlorn, wishing I was back out there on the road where my heart was. On the other hand, a tiny voice reminded me about the fatigue, the uncertainty, the hostels, the snoring at night, the lack of comfort and the being out in all weathers – things I wouldn't miss.

I left my backpack at reception and went out to wait for José. I wondered would I be back this way again, and whether I would ever hoist this pack for another day's walking on the Camino. My only hope was that, like Ignatius, this injury would mean something greater, a bigger plan over which I had no control.[40]

Solitary Confinement

The E-804 highway proved very noisy and very fast. Driving an old battered Renault, José, my Jesuit friend, ran a deluge of questions in Spanish past me. It was lovely to see him but I struggled to adjust to this radically different environment of overpasses, traffic lanes and speeding cars. There was not one hiker to be seen. Ironically, after all the sweat and toil that I had put into the twelve days of walking to Bilbao, the same distance would now be covered in little over an hour. It felt like cheating somehow and it was disorientating: all my normal referents of *albergues*, yellow arrows (*flechas amarillas*), trails (*caminos*) and pilgrims (*peregrinos*) were absent. I missed my walking companions and felt as if I was betraying them, going off like this. The thought that this fast escape might be my only goodbye to them brought a lump to my throat.

There was nothing for it but to engage with my new situation as wholeheartedly as I could. I had made the best decision I could in Bilbao, to heal and rest, and rehashing it would be unhelpful and disruptive.[41] I turned to look at José more clearly; what a blessing it was to be rescued by a familiar face in another country. I had a great fondness for José, whom I had not seen for six years since we studied and worked together in Dublin. We had been students on the same theology programme and had lived close to each other south of the River Liffey. I had brought him on many sight-seeing trips in Ireland and now the situation was reversed. We had lots of stories to tell to bring each other up to date (*ponernos al día*). It turned out we were both engaged in youth work, and we quickly realised we could collaborate on some common projects. He remained silent as I told him the story of our family's loss and the reason for this Camino walk. He understood; I felt heard.[42]

Driving alongside the River Arlanzón, Burgos looked dry, hot and built up. It was a far cry from a mountain path in the Basque region. I really felt like I was back in civiliza-tion when I was shown to a single room with a bed and a sink. These were rare luxuries. There wasn't a bunk bed in sight, nor a communal shower. It felt strange to have blinds on the windows and to be living in the half-light of indoors. I jumped at the offer to wash all my (greying) clothes in a machine, my hand-washing not having been up to scratch. I was given a tour of the Jesuit school and it was strange being introduced by my title (*Padre Jesuita, capellán* – Jesuit priest, chaplain) and not just by my first name as on the Camino.

That night José invited me out for an ice cream with another Jesuit, an artist named Jaime.[43] Sitting in the main plaza, I was recounting my Camino adventure and how it had unfortunately been cut short by injury. Walking by the river on the way home, Jaime took me aside and explained that he too had experience of walking the Camino. 'Your injury …' he said, 'is actually part of the Camino; maybe the most important part.' Intrigued, I pressed him to say more. 'It's a process', he said, 'much more than a simple walk, and it's what happens interiorly [in your mental and spiritual being] that matters. It is not about simply walking the trail; many people do this and often learn nothing.' He continued, 'If you can embrace this seemingly negative experience of injury, you will get closer to the heart of the Camino.'

I really wanted to agree with him, but it seemed too much to hope that this setback could actually be something positive for me (many pilgrims give up at this point). Then he added these words: 'The Camino is actually more powerful than doing the Spiritual Exercises retreat of St Ignatius.'[44] Now this was something I hadn't heard before but it was exciting, directly naming my sixteenth-century guide. I asked, 'What was it about your Camino experience that made it the ultimate retreat?' But to my frustration, he just tapped his finger on the side of his nose. I would have to wait and see if his insight was really true. If it was, I was really only beginning. However, at that moment, my injury was the greatest test, infinitely more frustrating than actually walking the trail. Still, there was room for some deeper learning here, and it gave me new hope for my own journey.

The next day an architectural jewel bedazzled me. Turning a corner, I came upon the soaring thirteenth-century Gothic cathedral Santa María de Burgos. The flying buttresses, delicate arches and towers all gave it a sense of shimmering in the warm air. Its white ashlar masonry launched it skywards by the sharp contrast with its surroundings. In the nave, I was mesmerized by the transcendent effect of the light, a reddish pink radiance. The impossibly fine pillars drew my eyes upwards to discover the source of this light. Indeed, I had heard that Gothic architecture's purpose was to elevate the mind and spirit, to the contemplation of heavenly things. I could imagine Ignatius of Loyola having looked on this, head flung back as he gazed skywards,[45] although there is no evidence of him ever being here.

Coming back to earth from my heavenly trip, I came across a familiar scallop shell set into the pavement outside the cathedral. I had originally intended to get away from the Camino for a while but, of course, here I was right on the principal route, the *Camino Francés*. This French route runs right past the cathedral and within a few minutes I spotted a steady stream of pilgrims passing in different states of repair. I recognised the perspiring faces, the bulging backpacks, the grimaces and the giveaway limps. The intense heat, around 30 degrees Celsius, made for much tougher walking and confirmed my choice of the coastal route. Here, however, I was seized by a mad urge to introduce myself as a fellow pilgrim, even though I wasn't a pilgrim and had no gear. I identified so much with their endeavour and the significance of their slog. I wanted it so badly, I even thought briefly of continuing the French route from here. But I was still officially out of action.

The next day I woke with a sense of D-day: decision day about going back on the Camino. I had to know if my leg was healed. I decided to wear the backpack and practice on the stairs in the Jesuit residence. If I felt pain at all I promised myself that I would call it quits. To my great relief, even though there was soreness and a lot of sensitivity around the muscle next to the shin, there was no real pain. Even then, I knew that going ahead would be a calculated risk; there were so many things that could go wrong.

'What would Ignatius do?' I thought. I think he would have asked if I had taken the usual measures, such as seeking medical help and getting rest, which I had. He would have been concerned about inflicting permanent injury on myself, which seemed unlikely here. Finally, I knew too that my burning desire to return to the Camino could be misleading and that I needed to look more dispassionately at the issues.[46] These included managing my injury well, going gently, planning support along the way should it happen again, and trying to be free of the pressure from my sponsors and supporters. I took some time over the decision; there was a lot riding on it. At last clarity and peace came, and my heart fairly soared deciding that I would continue. This was not to be the end of the story.

Later that day, I took a bus from Burgos back to Bilbao and said *adios*[47] to my dear friend José. He had been so kind to me and had really helped me during a low point. As I was getting out of the car, he promised he would arrange for me to stay in other Jesuit houses on the route if I needed. On the bus out of Burgos I felt a mixture of emotions: sadness alternating with excitement and nervousness. On the edge of the city we crossed the *Camino Francés* and I could see it was fairly thronged with walkers in the afternoon heat. It confirmed my decision to go back to Bilbao and stay with the *Camino del Norte*, with which I had quite an affinity now. It was rough and ready but with a unique charm in its solitude. As the Basque Country crept into view, I was struck by how mountainous it was and also how green and temperate; I was hoping the Way would treat me well.

As soon as I stepped off the bus in Bilbao, a giant sign – '*Rebajas* [Sale] *50%*' – in the window of a hiking shop drew my attention. Involuntarily, I was drawn inside before I knew it. There were endless rows of shorts, shell layers and fleeces, not to mention ropes, boots and crampons. And there were brand new shiny hiking poles …. I wasn't even back on the Camino, and yet here I was in hiker heaven, surrounded by the best gear at a huge discount. Exhilarated, I raced around the aisles, checking prices and brands, and unintentionally knocked over some stands with my backpack. The salesperson was bearing down on me and I knew that my freedom would not be long-lived.

Then I had this moment. The most curious feeling came over me, like I was detached from my surroundings. A creeping calm seemed to whisper, 'You don't actually need any of this stuff, this merchandise', and 'This will not bring you any real pleasure or help your Camino.' A wave of relief washed over me, and the manic-like tension that had held me drained away. I happen to have a thing for outdoor shops, and I felt overrun by this desire. But here, seen through the Camino lens, this materialist impulse was clearly at odds with the simple hiker lifestyle.

Viscerally, I felt something clarify within me, like putting on new glasses. The fierce grip of possessing, of being attached to things, was released within me. Even from a practical point of view, I had carefully packed for the absolute minimum and I couldn't afford extras. So apart from possibly replacing the poles, which weren't essential, I already had everything I needed for daily living. Ignatius, the ultimate pilgrim, would have understood this completely: to be free of those things that hinder progress, especially unhelpful attachments.[48]

Surprisingly, my brother Donal had also been a great model for how to be free from possessions. He cared not for appearance nor for wealth; he would give away money, clothes, his car, his time, as casually as breathing. You merely had to say you liked a jacket of his and next thing it was yours, or that you needed a lift and he had his keys in hand. He had this beat-up Toyota car that he would leave unlocked, sometimes with the keys in it, inviting anyone who wanted to steal it. Travelling abroad with him was challenging as he would throw a few things in a bag and arrive at the airport at the last second. Nothing was planned or prepared for: he merely trusted that he would be looked after. He owned some apartments and made a point of having the mostly unlikely tenants, especially people in difficulty. Often, this chaotic approach would cause him all sorts of problems but it all came from Donal's deep desire to help others, to be free of material things and to live from the heart. I felt particularly close to him as I shouldered my pack.

I made my way out to the lovely fishing port of Castro-Urdiales on the outskirts of the city. The harbour was breath-taking with its boats and historic buildings. While waiting for the hostel to open I toured a lovely twelfth-century Gothic church, Santa María, and then visited the dramatic castle and lighthouse on the point. Walking the deserted boardwalk, I toyed with the idea of a swim. Suddenly, a huge St Bernard dog bounded up, jumping up on me playfully. Almost immediately, a young woman appeared with a boxer dog and the two dogs ferociously attacked each other. Terrified, the woman started screaming, 'Pull him off, get your dog away!', assuming I was the owner. Shocked at the speed of events, I was reluctant to get involved with this whirl of teeth and snapping jaws. Eventually, I managed to get the St Bernard away with a combination of shouting and cattle-herding moves. As the St Bernard bounded off over the rise, the young woman also disappeared; it was all over except my accelerated heartbeat. What just happened? Was this a test of my own freedom, my willingness to respond and get involved? I wasn't sure; a graphic image of canine violence was burned in my consciousness however. I walked around more cautiously all afternoon. Even with the rucksack my leg felt fine, though understandably tender. I intended to take the next stage at a much gentler pace.

The hostel was hard to find, way out on the edge of town. As I trudged along, the evening sky was illuminated with bonfires and fireworks marking the summer solstice and the feast of San Juan. Inside the *refugio* (refuge, basic hostel), I felt like a Camino rookie, I was so slow organising my bunk and gear. Convinced I would meet my friends from before, I was disappointed not to recognise anyone. My companions now were mainly taciturn Germans and Austrians. I found it hard to let go; I was stuck in expectations about what should be, another thing to let go of. Like good pilgrims we were all in bed by 10 p.m. for that crucial early start.

The following morning found me on the road at 6.30 a.m., slipping into the old routine like a glove. On the elevated coastal path the first light was sublime; the sun rose directly out of the sea and was diffused through a ribbon of clouds. My heart burned[49] with gratitude and anticipation. I thought, 'There is nowhere else I'd rather be in the world right now.' Even though my left leg was still tender and I walked gingerly, I prayed with emotion: 'This is enough for me.'[50] There was no one around to witness this historic moment: my second attempt at the Camino.

Fortunately, the route was fairly flat and well-paved as I meandered along the Cantabrian coast. At one stage I walked through a herd of goats, the brilliant sea immediately to my right and a huge mountain to the left. 'I will remember this moment forever', I thought. I was so happy; happy to be alive witnessing this magical coast, but also grateful I wasn't on a plane returning home. Each step became a treasured gift. I realised again the precariousness of this quest, that I might not finish the Camino at all or even get to the next village. Paradoxically, this thought freed me up, made me appreciate every little advance and made the moment precious. Knowing I couldn't control it helped me surrender to it more fully.

I arrived in Rioseco (Dry River) before noon and had a coffee at a bar with my own crudely made sandwiches. I had walked 13 kilometres without any problems, although most of it was flat, and it seemed a great achievement. Looking ahead at the afternoon section, the map showed an uphill route. Not wanting to push my leg too hard, I decided to bypass the mountain by taking a 20-minute bus ride instead. The woman behind the bar was extremely helpful, but I was disappointed to find that the next bus would not depart for another four hours. Looking at the map I thought I found an alternative route. I set off in the wrong direction however, and 2 kilometres later a man in a wheelchair informed me I had gone totally the wrong way. There was nothing for it but return to the bar and await the bus. At least there was shade to prevent me melting in the afternoon heat. I also had time to reflect on the day: great initially and then I got off track later; I really felt I was a slow learner. However, I had a very strong sense that I was being taught through all these detours and injuries. Mostly I needed to slow down and be more patient, accepting the gift inherent in a situation without looking to better it.

It was early evening when I arrived in Laredo, very late for the hostels. As places were in short supply, four other German pilgrims from the bus and I made a beeline for the tourist office. I found a hostel nearby, El Buen Pastor, run by the Good Shepherd sisters. Having both single and double

rooms, the hostel was a notch above any other and accord-
ingly more expensive. After trekking up and down corridors
with a flustered nun, it transpired that all the rooms were
taken. Explaining that I was a Jesuit priest helped thaw out
the stress I had caused her and seemed to give her an idea. So
after a delay, she came back to tell me that she had organised
a room for me with the Trinitarian nuns, an enclosed order,
in St Francis' Convent nearby.

Tired by now, I walked slowly over to the imposing
convent door; after ringing the bell, the door sprung open
remotely. I climbed the silent monastery stairs with some
anticipation, and was met by a ruddy-faced nun in full habit.
Wordlessly, she brought me to an isolated bedsit in a corner
of the monastery. Gesturing for my *credencial*, she stamped
it. I paid her the room fee of €10 and off she glided into the
cloister. The silence, far from awkward, was liberating. The
Camino had taught me the value of that. I studied my unique
stamp, '*Monjas Trinitarias – Laredo*', with delight. Quite a
boon, this room turned out to be much better lodgings than
I could have imagined. Though there were no windows
and the bathroom was so small I couldn't do laundry, I was
appreciative of what I had. I ignored all the dead mosquitoes
on the walls, which wouldn't have helped peaceful slumber.
Having reflected on a good day, I slept very well. Like a monk
in a silent monastery, I enjoyed my solitary confinement.

Too Much of a Good Thing

Back in the seaside town of Laredo, the deadly drone of a mosquito impelled me to rise. I guessed that it had already bitten me and this would manifest as an irritating scratch later. I knew now why the room was plastered with dead mosquitoes. There was no food included in this unique monastery deal so after packing I headed straight to the expansive surf beach. Lined with hotels and apartments, it was deserted at this early hour and I had the sandy wilderness all to myself. At the end of the shore was a ferry across to another town, Santoña, which would save me a lot of walking. Ahead of me stretched a vast sand flat, a great crescent that swept around into a rocky headland, resplendent in a perfect sunrise.

Leaning into the stiff breeze, I hugged myself with glee, delightedly savouring this desolate moment. Hungry for breakfast, I scanned the ragged line of bars and hotels that ringed the beach. A lone walker told me that nothing was open and to follow the beach right around the point for the ferry. This took me well over an hour, particularly as there was no indication where the ferry pulled in. As I was early, I sat on a sandy shelf and was delighted to discover some fruit and chocolate in my backpack.

The ferry, more like a glorified launch, ploughed straight into the shore to make a gangway for the ten or so people waiting. Hearing the accents, I picked out two young Irish women, Carol and Fiona, teachers on their first Camino experience. Over coffee on Santoña's promenade, we swapped stories. Kitted out in brand new gear, they were taking a week on the northern route and then going south for a beach holiday. It quickly transpired that they were rookies on the Camino and were finding it very tough, especially as their priority was to have a holiday. I found myself in the unlikely role of the 'seasoned veteran', having been on the Camino for longer than them. I had a lot of sympathy for them, and gladly gave them all of my hard-earned tips. However, I felt that it wouldn't be long before they called it a day. Afterwards I was reflecting on what a crucial role motivation plays, and how the Camino really tests people. It is a fire that purifies commitment, determining how much people want to do it. For these women it determined how the walk was experienced – that is, punishing as opposed to enjoyable. The same experience of hostels, basic facilities, strenuous exercise and mediocre food can be interpreted in vastly different ways.[51]

The typical Camino image is one of trails and hills, but from Laredo on it was mostly beach walking. Walking along a pristine sandy beach by a whispering ocean, I almost felt guilty relishing the experience. Having had my fill of mud, forest and mountain, here was dramatic coastal scenery more befitting vacationers. Almost immediately I came on the unspoilt beach of Berria, which was empty except for a few walkers, surfers and fishermen. The Camino route ran parallel with the beach and it seemed infinitely preferable to walk on the sand, enjoying the beach vistas and windblown casualness. I was sorry to come onto a headland where I had to climb cautiously while protecting my leg.

However, this was not the end; the view further down the coast revealed a string of indented sandy shores. Directly in front of me was the thronged, touristy beach at Helgueras.

Even though it was scarred with rocky veins, it was another sandy haven, open to the turquoise sea and sky. There were people everywhere – swimming, picnicking, walking and playing games. It was a strange contrast between the holiday-makers in swimwear and the line of hikers cutting a swathe through them. Distinctive with their backpacks, poles and sunhats, the walkers stood out. They strode with military intensity and purpose in mountain boots, paying little attention to the relaxation and fun around them. I stopped for lunch at a rocky outcrop and threw off my gear to temporarily at least enjoy some beach atmosphere.

Just when it seemed that this seaside delight would never finish, at Trengandín beach near Noja, the Camino took a turn inland. I was fortunate to fall in with a group of Dutch people and a lone Spanish woman, as I was lost. Incredibly, there were no more yellow arrows on the road and my guidebook was vague and useless. In a roadside huddle we realised we were lost, none of the guidebooks providing clear direction. I was mightily relieved when a young Dutch woman took the lead and confidently directed us for many kilometres through a maze of roads and paths. At one point we had to cross a salt marsh and passed some stone water mills on a tidal estuary. This was all an act of trust as there were no signs and no real landmarks. On and on we went through nondescript lanes, valleys and fields. At one stage a huge eagle pounced on some prey right beside me, an eerie reminder not to get separated from the group.

The Spanish woman started to lag behind and the Dutch woman, with admirable patience, had us all wait for her. I observed the Spanish woman catch up with us; she was strolling along nonchalantly, her backpack on one shoulder, talking loudly on the phone and smoking a cigarette. It seemed the epitome of relaxed style, but there was something that didn't quite fit, something out of balance. On reaching us, the Spanish woman lost her temper, asking whose idea was this route, and complaining that she should have known better, that she always preferred to go on her own. Patiently, the Dutch woman showed her where we were on the map, assuring her we were not lost. It was a model of how to deal with a difficult person using compassion and kindness. I doubted that I would have been able to see the positive side and react to her so well.[52]

We stopped at a hillside bar for some ice cream where the Spanish woman again took an inordinate amount of time. The Dutch woman made sure she knew where we were going and what the route was, and we left her there. We breathed a collective sigh of relief, and the rest of us began making more progress. Little did I realise I would be meeting her again soon.

We were in rolling Cantabrian farming country, patch-work crops and forest, but the throbbing in my feet made it hard to think of anything else. We walked through a pass in the mountains and then into another valley where the famil-iar yellow arrows again pointed the way. At my limit, I was so glad to see the signs for the hostel and appreciative of the Dutch group for their company and guidance.

Arriving in Güemes, we could be forgiven for thinking we had arrived in paradise. There were people to greet us when we arrived, water and fruit to eat as we sat down, and excep-tional hospitality from volunteers[53] who, as former pilgrims, knew what it was like to arrive footsore and hungry. The Güemes hostel, La Cabana del Abuelo Peuto, was on a hill-top, was custom-made for hikers and had lots of bright, airy rooms. After I signed in, an eager volunteer brought me on a tour and showed me to my spacious bunkroom. Afterwards, I was invited to a communal dinner made by the volunteer *hos-pitaleros*. Incredibly, they only asked for a voluntary donation to cover all. It was a radical departure from the minimalistic *albergues* in which I had previously stayed.

That night the head *hospitalero* called all the walkers together for what was a first for me: a briefing on the next day's walk. I was volunteered as the English translator. He had a map displayed of the next *etapa*, which would finish in the great city of Santander, but there was a choice of routes: a direct road route or a longer coastal path. Afterwards, someone took out a guitar and some wine, and we had a great sing-along, which I couldn't resist contributing to. This was what I had missed in other hostels – a strong sense of community, fun and sharing. As I lay in my bunk, content with the full day, there was quite a lot to reflect on. I made a note in my blog: 'Possibly the best hostel I've stayed in: a rare combination of eating together, talking and sharing experiences.' Someone had told me this community experience was much more typical of the *Camino Francés* hostels.

I woke to a cold and crisp morning, perfect walking weather. I made a point of saying goodbye to the volunteers and the distinctive *albergue* in Güemes. As I marched down the country road, I fell into step with Willy, a German man I had met the previous night. He was tall and thin, wearing round horn-rimmed glasses and had no hat, which made him squint in the strong sunlight. We had no common language but he had an amazing knack of communicating with whistles and gestures that was endearing. Eventually we came to a major road and the choice of routes we had been told about; the advantages of the coastal route readily convinced us though it was considerably longer.

Shortly we came to some sheer cliffs with a trail right along the edge. The view of isolated beaches, blue-green ocean and clear sky was intoxicating. The morning mist clung to the contours of the receding cliffs, reinforcing the silence that held us spellbound. The pristine Cantabrian coastline spoke of the beauty of creation. Looking back, there was a line of some twenty pilgrims on the same route. Eventually they caught up with us and, rather than race ahead, we let them go, finding a dramatic clifftop eyrie where we could contemplate the vast seascape below.

Eventually we rejoined the trail and met a number of young Germans, one of whom seemed to be leading the way. I recognised him from the briefing the night before where he had also been helping with the translation. We came again to a decision point where the Camino headed inland but there was a rough path along the rocky shore. Instinctively I plunged ahead following the coast, but shortly we came to a rocky headland that was difficult to scale with backpacks. The young German man remonstrated with me for disobeying the guidebook and taking a wrong turn. I was beyond caring about the book at this stage; I could smell the sea and I wanted to be close to it.

Eventually we came to a famous surf beach, Arenal del Puntal, and were back among dozens of holidaymakers. The hard, wet sand was a pleasure to hike along and the noise of the breakers was hypnotic. Willy and I stopped for a snack in the shade of some boulders; he had a stove for brewing tea, a rare luxury. Another 40 minutes brought us to the town of Somo and a short sprint brought us across a sandy spit and to the ferry for Santander. Being on the boat felt like a treat, resting our legs and being swept across the sea. It was exhilarating sweeping into the huge port of Santander imagining what it would have been like for pilgrims arriving centuries ago.

Our group of hikers went straight to the tourist office to get maps and find the location of the hostels, and then we sought out the Gothic Catedral de Nuestra Señora de la Asunción. Our timing was perfect as inside the sun was streaming in through the columns in the old cloister. The interplay of light and stone in honeyed hues was inspiration designed for a medieval monk. The main cathedral was packed with clergy, dignitaries and worshippers for the celebration of Corpus Christi. After celebrating Mass there was an elaborate procession around the city, which the Spanish excel at. Seeing the Blessed Sacrament on the move, I had a curious feeling of walking with the pilgrim Christ, who was my guide on this journey, even though often I couldn't see too far ahead.

Now mid-afternoon, the other hikers tried persuading me to accompany them to the hostel. Stubbornly I refused, insisting I had to get out of the city, into the country and make up lost time. Alone again, I took a metro to the suburbs and got off where the city ran out. Immediately, I met an Italian couple who had booked a hotel on the Camino and were fretfully trying to find it. I found myself getting caught up in their anxiety. Initially, they helped me greatly in getting on track but afterwards I was left with a heavy heart; maybe I should have stayed with them, taken the easy option? Without any clear destination, I continued my solitary trudge uphill. I had an uneasy sense that I had misplaced or missed something important.

I toiled up an endless hill in the oppressive afternoon heat, eventually coming on the hilltop village of Mogro, little more than a church and a square. My guidebook stated that the parish priest of the local church, San Martín, was very welcoming to pilgrims and that there was some makeshift accommodation at the church. However, when I asked next door they told me that the priest had moved and that he only came on Sundays for Mass. They did offer to open the church porch for me however, and let me take a siesta there to get over the worst of the heat. The flagstones were delicious – a cool remedy for the feet – and the concrete bench was like a feather bed. After an hour's rest, I reluctantly set off again in the intense heat, getting more and more ill-tempered as sweat obscured my vision and blisters began to make their presence felt.

I was now committed to walking across an arid hill to Polanco, an industrial area, where I knew there was a municipal hostel. This was exactly the situation I didn't want to be in – caught out between hostels, having to walk on asphalt in the searing heat. I began to limp; blisters were hurting my feet and I could find no relief from the 30-degree heat. By now far from the coast, all the inspiring seascapes were gone; burnt grass and dust predominated. It turned into a grim marathon; I was regretting my decision to push on.

Even though I had thought continuing was the best option and had justified it to myself, I felt deceived and almost betrayed.[54] The good that I sought turned out to be only 'apparent' or misleading. It was painfully obvious to me how important Ignatius' notion of 'balance'[55] was; how a seemingly good desire can become distorted and bring me in the opposite direction. An image formed inside my head of a weighing scale or spinning top being tipped out of balance by excess weight or pressure. Ignatius of Loyola knew this through bitter experience, suffering the ravages of his own extreme behaviour, attachments and destructive impulses. That was the crucible in which balance was forged.[56]

I had seen this same dynamic in Donal. His passion and great love of life sometimes got turned against himself. There seemed to be some malign spirit undermining his talent for helping others, making friends and enjoying himself. Being totally available and trying to please others often brought him to great sadness and depression. He was too good for his own good, as we said at his funeral. I could see something similar working in me now: being seduced by something that seemed good (walking further), but was actually damaging.[57] How had I been led so far off track, off balance? I realised that I had exceeded my body's limits, overriding my earlier 'take it easy' wisdom. I had wrongly prioritised getting out of the city over rest and recovery. Simply accepting the mild inconvenience of a city hostel, one night in an urban context, would have saved me a lot of pain.

Ignatius had this great rule of thumb[58] about decisions: even though something seems obvious and straightforward and may have worked before, you have to examine it carefully and pray it through to ensure it is genuinely good. Something clearly negative is easy to spot, but that which appears good on the surface, a subtle form of deception, can be misleading. Ignatius called this the deception of the 'Angel of Light',[59] or how we get derailed by *apparent* goods. He designed a canny method for thoroughly examining 'attractive' ideas to uncover hidden traps, something I would remember.[60] I had lost my balance,[61] to use Ignatius' metaphor, and I had learned a valuable lesson, but it was just a temporary setback if I could recover my poise and get back on track. Wearily, I resolved to make the most of it.

One man stopped his car to give me directions; I craved the air-conditioned coolness within. A number of other people were also very helpful on the road, but I was grimly hanging on. I hobbled into Polanco in the late afternoon and found the Quin Bar (short for 'Joaquin'). A kind elderly woman, Señora Ascensión, gave me the keys and indicated the *albergue* a further 500 metres down the road in a small depression. I thought she was mistaken at first; it looked like an electricity sub-station or a low barn. She showed me into what was possibly the unlikeliest hostel in the world, with only two narrow rooms and three bunks in each. An Italian couple had taken one room so I had the other to myself.

To get inside away from the heat was an enormous relief. Bathed in sweat and with my feet throbbing, I collapsed into a chair and had a cold soft drink; every tangy drop tasted like heaven. I had a go at puncturing my blisters but ended up making a mess of them. Entering the shower, the floor was swimming in water, with soap scum and human hair everywhere. There was nothing for it but to delicately tiptoe over and get under the cold water quickly. Coming back to my bunk, I noticed that the covers on the beds, though once cream, were now something of a smoky brown.

I dreaded going back up to the bar for food, but I had no choice; there was nowhere else to go in this factory zone. The señora brought me into a side room off the bar; there was no one else there. I was offered a great deal – three courses for €9; hunger negated all thoughts about it being hygienic. The salad was a bit tired and the spaghetti lame, but I ate and enjoyed it all. Coming back to the micro-hostel, the two Italians were asleep and I was a dead man walking. Entombed in the oppressive heat, I was so tired I slept eventually.

6

Walking on Broken Glass

Dawn came as an unwelcome guest in the distinctly shabby Polanco hostel. I tried keeping my eyes shut for as long as possible, putting off the moment when I would have to face reality again. The hostel didn't improve in daylight and, though I was trying to make the best of it, it was hard not to see the squalor in the dirt and chaos. Arriving uninvited came the thought 'The worst hostel I have stayed in', but I resisted breaking the Camino rule about being ungrateful for anything. This simple rule had served me well and it left me free to accept whatever else, good or bad, was coming down the line.[62] This place had provided me with food and shelter at one of my worst moments; it was a timely refuge.[63] I briefly considered staying on in the *albergue* and getting medical help but I knew that pilgrims could only stay one night per hostel. The Italian couple next door had gone without a sound and I hadn't even spoken a word to them. I made an equally silent and rapid exit from this timely but grubby shelter, which had served me well despite my grumblings. I said a little prayer of gratitude and touched the lintel as I left.[64]

Then the pain began as I hoisted the backpack and my feet engaged the pavement. I had almost forgotten about the blisters, presuming that like most problems they would be cured by sleep and rest. They were back with a vengeance however, now with a jangly nerve pain that spoke of cracked and torn skin. The experience was akin to walking on broken glass in bare feet. Feeling even more of a fool for having overdone it the day before, I was determined to walk through it and put it behind me. 'Sometimes the start is the worst', I told myself, and set about gritting my teeth and ignoring the pain. Seeking distraction, I looked to either side but there were only deserted rows of warehouses, electrical pylons and car parks. It felt like I was lost in a featureless industrial zone, with few signs of human habitation and deprived of nature's transcendent beauty. The bleak environment echoed my inner world like some dreadful pathetic fallacy, where the emotions shape the surroundings.

One foot having become unbearably painful, I sought to favour the other and limping along with the rucksack became progressively harder. Hungry, I was holding out for a café or bar to have breakfast and get relief from the pain to assess the situation. Normally I would have brought some food from the night before but there had been nothing available. It was exactly 7 a.m. when I came upon a bar full of builders and truckers. The décor was very 1970s minimalism and macho functionalism. A backpack, shorts and sunhat were suddenly incongruous. Grimacing on my way to the bar to order, I knew instinctively that I wouldn't be walking much further that day. The pain from the broken blisters was much more acute than the day before and I dared not take off my socks to look at them. A lame hiker stranded between worlds, I found a remote window table with a view of van roofs and trucks. I spread out my map on the Formica table in the vain hope of examining what few options were left to me.

Failing to work its normal magic, coffee and a croissant brought no tangible relief. What weighed heaviest was the knowledge that I had to get away from this predominantly commercial area and get some urgent medical attention; I had to step off the Camino again and all that went with it. Integrating that decision and acting upon it was still beyond me however – I needed time to work through all the false voices and inner critics that would have me ignore the problem and keep going. I could hear a voice admonishing me for failing again, betraying my mission and taking the 'easy way out'. It was an inner war of emotion, differing desires and conflicting motivations. I had to sit tight and wait out the storm, the true desires revealing themselves with time.[65] Getting help, though humbling, was the right thing to do. Getting back on the Camino was up in the air.

Sitting at that table was a real low point as I could see the Camino recede from me again, ruled out by my own rashness and misplaced zeal. Some time later I came to the necessary decision to ask the barman for the nearest doctor and he told me how to catch a bus there. I got directions to the bus stop, which was still a considerable walk involving a certain amount of pain. I was feeling much better however, having a clear purpose.[66] As I came to the indicated twin roundabouts, I reflected how little beauty there was to them. I ignored my normal routine of applying sunscreen and putting on my hat; 'I won't need those any more', I thought. At the main highway, I found the bus stop beside a dilapidated church. 'Where was God in this experience of humiliating defeat?'[67] I wondered, fed up with this second major setback. I boarded the bus for the short journey to Santillana del Mar, where I would get medical attention. It was still only 9 a.m. and I was done for the day, maybe for the whole Camino.

I was so fed up I hardly noticed the medieval stone buildings, the historic centre and the many tourists in Santillana. I alighted beside the Santa Clara Convent, an endearing building in terracotta and sandstone. I briefly toyed with whether I would throw myself on their mercy, like a poor wounded medieval pilgrim, seeking sanctuary to heal and recover. Dismissing that idea, I set about finding the medical centre, which was only metres from where the bus left me.

Santillana's *consultorio médico* was in a low brownstone building. Fortified by my positive medical experience in Bilbao, I expectantly joined the queue. It quickly became apparent, however, that this would be a very different experience.

A stressed secretary was struggling to cope with the swelling numbers. She was getting frustrated with her computer and with those in front of her. In turn, people were getting very impatient, gesturing and protesting. I could see this coming down the line as I drew closer: the foreigner without proper documents who was going to cause an even bigger hold-up. Sure enough, I was met by a wall of irritation and short-temperedness, implying that I was causing great annoyance. I asked Ignatius to give me strength for this particular ordeal.[68] It took all my reserves of patience and compassion, all the while with feet on fire, to go through the extensive paperwork, fend off the emotional undertow and not respond in kind. It was over an hour before I got my appointment as first I had to go to a nearby bank to pay a fee into their account before they would see me.

Coming into the surgery was like entering a different world of tranquillity, peace and order. The doctor was kind and efficient and after a brief look passed me on to a nurse who injected the blisters with some kind of disinfectant. She put two white chunky pads over the balls of my feet, telling me to rest for at least one day minimum. Walking out, I felt like I was floating on air with the pain largely gone. Being treated medically was one thing, but what was invaluable was having the problem solved and being offered the hope of continuing the Camino. I treated myself to a cheap room in a boarding house (*posada*), marvelling at the delights of a single room, and immediately enjoyed a two-hour siesta in clean sheets, a rare luxury.

Now that I had time, well-being and sanity, I was able to explore the considerable delights of the town, with extensive stonework dating from the fourteenth to the eighteenth centuries. The little narrow streets with quaint balconies harked

back to a different era, and the buildings lining them had
now been reinvented as craft shops and hotels. I attended a
high Mass in the historic twelfth-century Santa Juliana collegiate church, celebrated by an Italian priest who was in
a constant fight with the Spanish language. Afterwards, I
called into the hostel at the other end of town and met some
brash young German walkers from a few days ago, but no
one else I knew.

After a bite to eat in a friendly café on the edge of town, I
went back to the *posada*. The quiet park in front of my room
had been transformed with a stage, rides and food stalls.
There was a salsa concert complete with glittery costumes
and theatrical smoke in full swing outside my *posada*. I discovered it was a fiesta in honour of the town's patron, Santa
Juliana, whose feast was the next day. At the foot of the
stage I was glued to the spot soaking up the lights, colours,
music and dance, a celebration of Cantabrian culture. I felt
like I had been deprived of such joys on the ascetic Camino.
Fatigue eventually forced me away; it had been a long day of
many twists and turns. My reflection was short and sweet;
sleep came easily.

Waking late, I stumbled down to a very meagre continen-
tal breakfast, not a fried egg in sight. This, the actual feast
day of Santa Juliana, was another day of fiesta beginning
with a solemn Mass and procession in her honour. The cobbled streets leading up to the church were filled with brightly
coloured traditional dresses and groups of men carried life-
size statues, including ones of Saint Juliana, up the middle of
the street. A great group of clergy and acolytes in robes and
lace added to the drama. I had never seen such pomp and
pageantry – the elaborate costumes, the marching bands, the
banners and flags, a huge standard bearing the saint's image,
and all topped off with extensive fireworks.

Just before Mass I spotted my friend Willy from a few days
ago coming into town enveloped in plastic because of the
rain. I was really delighted to see him and we chatted briefly

in our unique sign language before he had to go on. 'We'll have a beer in Finisterre at the Camino's end', he shouted as he walked away. Watching him go left me disconsolate; it reinforced the fact that I was presently unable to walk. I was left alone with little to do for the whole day, especially after the morning's excitement. The boarding house offered no solace: the bedroom a dull floral print room whose windows opened onto brick walls, I could have been anywhere in the world.

The afternoon was completely rained out and I chose to walk the short distance out of town to the zoo as a distraction. I also wanted to test how my feet were holding up and, promisingly, they seemed better. I felt curiously unbalanced walking on a road without my pack, like a fundamental part of me was missing. The rain was bouncing off the road and all the vegetation was sagging under its weight. Located on the side of a ravine, the zoo was home to hundreds of species under a canopy of thick vegetation. However, with the dismal day, all the animals looked pathetic and miserable, and this didn't help my mood much. I made a beeline for the brown bear enclosure, to admire these great North American beasts. One of them kept making desperate attempts to escape, swinging right up the side of the enclosure. It was distressing, the enforced captivity of a wild creature in a steel cage. Even worse, the other bears had simply given in to immobility, apathetically resigned to their fate.

The lethargic bears struck me as an image for Donal's depression, being unable to cope and tuning out of the world into an alternate reality. I remember when things had come to a head some twenty years previously and I took time off from my job in England to help my brother in his crisis. Taking on too much, ignoring accumulated stress and not having an emotional safety valve had created an emergency situation for him. Even getting the help of a specialist and medication did little to take the edge off it. It was to be the beginning of a drift over two decades that scarcely registered initially, but which ossified over time and gradually eroded the spaces for healthy living.

Distressing for me was watching this unfold in a person I loved while knowing that solutions were possible. I and many of my siblings, some of them experienced health professionals, were powerless to act and could only watch this tragedy unfold with some horror. I had written before that Donal 'drowned in a pool full of lifeguards'[69] and it was utterly devastating to be left as a rescuer with a slack rope, all attempts at rescue having failed. Particularly cruel was that the summer before his death, Donal miraculously appeared to be back to his positive self and on the mend. But instead of recovery this was rather a common warning sign of imminent suicide that should have set off alarm bells. I so much wanted to believe that the tide was turning and that rescue was imminent. Blinded by intense desire, I misread the signs and reaped a harvest of regrets. I realised now, on a rainy hillside in Santillana del Mar, that letting go of the terrorism of 'shoulds' and allowing self-forgiveness was the journey that I needed to walk. I still had a ways to go.

The tropical butterfly house I stumbled upon next was a joy though, with its hot and steamy climate. There I was surrounded by thousands of delicate furry wings flying over and around me, with many landing on my clothes. Turquoise, gold and yellow wings of impossible fragility flew playfully around a host of tropical plants. I felt like I had been transported to a parallel dream world of vivid colour, delicacy and beauty. The Camino appeared hard, drab and uninviting in contrast. I fantasised about the prospect of remaining wrapped in this sultry cocoon, immobile and safe, but like the bears I knew this was not the place for me. The only bars preventing me from escape were those in my own head: fears, exaggerations and doubts. The idea of giving up was preying on my mind at this stage, but I knew that I had to act against it.

The lethargy of the bears, the seductive deception of Donal's seeming recovery and now my own resignation at another setback all seemed to point towards a subtle but destructive negativity. Depression particularly has an insidious reasoning that justifies inactivity, withdrawal and poisonous rumination. Even though it feels like the opposite of what you want to do, the answer is to act against these instincts, get going, engage and crawl out from under the cloud. Ignatius of Loyola knew this counter-intuitive dynamic well – it wasn't just about acting when feeling good, sometimes he had to galvanise himself into action. This was about digging deep in difficult moments, resisting easy solutions and getting back on track. Ignatius called this challenging approach 'acting against';[70] at times when you are in a rut, lazy or in desolation you have to act against the way you feel and take decisive steps to get back on course. I really wished that Donal could have profited from this wisdom, to act against his demons, face down the insidious deceptions and make those crucial, courageous decisions. I wanted him to be a free butterfly and not a caged bear, but he wasn't able to make the transformation for a whole host of reasons, many beyond his control. I needed to forgive him too.

The experience crystallized my desire to get back on the trail the next day – I had to act against an encroaching negativity that would have me surrender and give in. Sitting around would not address the situation but walking carefully would. I decided to do whatever distance I could reasonably do the next day, starting off walking slowly and observing my limits. I was glad for the blessings of a day of reflection;[71] even though challenging, I had a new clarity and focus. It seemed increasingly clear to me that I had to learn a few lessons about taking it easy, not walking in the heat and lowering expectations.

Get Out of Jail

It wasn't even light when I walked out of Santillana, anxious to get moving. The last two days seemed like a dark chapter that I wanted to forget: blisters and boarding houses. With every step my heart lifted and I was glad to be back on the road again, a pilgrim. I felt free and alive, the blisters healed and forgotten. I really needed to believe this was a new start, getting over the indignity of being immobilised. Fortunately, it was quite an easy, flat road walk at this stage and the big mountains of the Basque Country were a distant memory. It started to rain though, drizzling at first and then coming down more consistently. I was forced to dig out my DayGlo cape, which the wind instantly made into a sail. With the clouds and weather down it was a dull landscape, the telegraph poles scraping a low grey sky.

Once again I hadn't managed to get any breakfast before I left and was very quickly running on empty. I walked on through several drab Cantabrian villages showing no sign of life. With the rain dripping off my cape, I made it into an unremarkable coffee shop in a town called Cóbreces around 9 a.m. I was amazed to meet there the stroppy Spanish woman of the 'lost' crisis a few days earlier and a Dutch guy who had been there too. Spontaneously I was glad to see some familiar faces and I felt among friends. Normally I walked alone, but that day I needed some company. We ordered some *café con leche*, toast and eggs and sat in the half-light by the door as the rain continued to fall outside.

My companions had just arisen from the nearby hostel and were having a leisurely morning. As we were catching up, I recounted the story of my adventures so far: my forced stay in Santillana del Mar and having to take the bus. Immediately I could tell they weren't impressed. In fact, the Spanish woman had a bit of an edge to her voice as she chastised me about deviating from the Camino and taking shortcuts. It was the 'Camino purist' ethic[72] in its classic form and I found myself reacting to her hostility. I was a bit taken aback; I felt some defensiveness and frustration at being challenged, but mostly I felt knocked off my game. I realised that I had to change strategy rapidly to avoid getting pulled into her agenda.[73] She became more strident, insisting that I should withdraw from the Camino, that I wasn't experienced enough and that I would not be able to finish it. I couldn't believe what I was hearing from a fellow pilgrim. Instinctively, I knew that I had to dig deep[74] to maintain my balance and fend off this attack, which came at a low moment. After taking a moment to collect myself, conscious that I did not want to react in a similarly angry way, I merely replied, 'There are many different Caminos', an intriguing phrase I had heard used by Camino walkers to describe the uniqueness of each person's journey. I had to repeat this several times, like a broken record, to shake her off her 'evangelical' pedestal.

To add salt to the wound, the Dutch guy chipped in that he thought there was something wrong with my shoes; he had noticed my right foot was turning outwards when he was walking behind me a few days previously. I thanked him for this observation (which was to prove useful later). Eventually we came to a conversational impasse with a certain lack of common ground. They donned their rain gear and headed off for San Vincente, some 15 kilometres away. I was glad to see them gone all right, but it took a while to shake off the resentment and be free of it.[75] I had a *pan dulce* and an extra coffee to calm myself, feeling shaken by this unexpected emotional tsunami.

Galvanising myself into action, I had a look around the rest of the town, which was only a thin strip of buildings up the side of a hill. One building stood out immediately however, a freshly painted Cistercian abbey, the Abadía de Santa María de Viaceli. I was used to churches and abbeys being deserted, but on inspecting the notice board I discovered that there was an active community of around thirty monks here, and that mid-morning prayer was currently in progress. There was a sign on the door that said 'Do not enter during prayer times', but I considered this a spiritual emergency, given the morning I had had. It was with great delight that I sneaked (noisily with my rucksack) into the Cistercians' inner sanctum. Thankfully the monks and other people praying gave me only the slightest of glances; it was a welcome refuge of light and warmth on what had been a mean, wet day. Even though I couldn't follow the prayers, being there was enough for me. Simply being physically present, and showing up, was enough. I gave thanks for having survived my hardest test yet and for the hard-won wisdom. As I came out, the rain had stopped and hope sprung anew in my heart: I was still on course to Santiago despite the obstacles.

The weather started to improve and as I took off my rain cape the sun struggled out from its leaden prison. I slipped into that lovely but elusive rhythm which makes walking effortless. Gradually things swam back into focus after the difficult morning, walking being the best way to process and integrate what had happened.[76] Ironically, the earlier conflict had galvanised my determination to walk at my own pace, which was 'in a relaxed manner'.[77] I purposefully took my time and enjoyed every detail, even though my feet began to hurt again. Fortunately I was close to Comillas, my destination for the day, and I could see the coast again. Tramping along the Bay of Biscay, I breathed deeply and loved being alive.

The town's famous crescent beach was that day, however, damp and uninviting. I entered the historic and picturesque town of Comillas by the main square. What first caught my eye was the cemetery protected by an imposing marble angel. The woman in the tourist office kindly let me leave my rucksack in her office, the hostel not being open yet. After having a local dish of fried eggs and bacon in a café seemingly hewn from the sandstone rock, I set about exploring this Roman town.

Comillas is rich in history and different layers of civilization are written into its very walls. I was really taken with the main church, San Cristóbal, the seventeenth-century exterior of which was dramatically crumbling away to reveal a variety of stone and brick surfaces. I continued my architectural stroll around the neo-Gothic Sobrellano Palace, the grim exterminator angel looking over the cemetery and Gaudi's folly, a modernist mix of bizarre shapes and styles. As the sun descended I walked around the scenic port and wondered at some ominously high mountains on the horizon.

I raced back to the hostel for its 4 p.m. opening but there was already quite a queue there. The hostel was a rugged square stone building and the windows had obviously been a recent addition in what would have been blank walls. I discovered it had been the town's eighteenth-century jail – I would have cause to remember this later.

Queuing up for an *albergue* bed is a great leveller; people naturally fall into conversation with one another. I greeted the pilgrim behind me and within a few minutes we were talking like intimates. He also was a priest and though he was Spanish, he worked in Peru. Miguel had been trained by the Jesuits in Madrid and so we had a lot of common ground right away. He asked me if I had celebrated Mass that day

(I hadn't) and invited me to accompany him to the local church to ask if we could concelebrate. Ditching my rucksack on a bed, I was happy to go with him.

Within minutes we were back at the church of San Cristóbal (of the crumbling walls) and as it was the feast day of their patron, San Pedro el Pescador, the pews were packed. As we strode up the main aisle, my eyes were captivated by the huge pillars that soared up into a Gothic ceiling. I admired Miguel's confidence as he strode assuredly into the sacristy and presented us as a liturgical team. The parish priest seemed happy at the offer and asked us to lead the whole evening's Mass. The next thing I knew Miguel was dividing up the liturgical tasks, inviting me to preach the homily on the Gospel. I baulked at this, knowing my Spanish, while good, would not stretch to that without serious preparation.

In the end Miguel was the main celebrant, and I read the Gospel. I knew Miguel was the right man for preaching when I saw him hold the whole congregation in rapt attention, effortlessly ad libbing like an old hand. I had a vision of St Peter evangelising the Gentiles, full of zeal and conviction, such was his passion and presence. Just when I thought all was over, it transpired that there was also a Eucharistic procession around the village afterwards, complete with band, singers and dancers. We were the principal dignitaries. Every few minutes the procession would stop in the thronged village square and the dancers would twirl as fireworks were set off. It was then that I caught the eyes of some of our fellow pilgrims from the hostel among the crowd who were incredulous at our presence there. Afterwards Miguel and I had a simple meal of fried mackerel and bread with a glass of wine as we unwound from a hectic day. On the way back to the hostel we paused by a stone cross set high above the town just as the sun was setting over the ocean. I was touched by beauty and heart-wrenching sadness; I thought of how Donal would have loved to have shared this moment, this 'spiritual peak' moment.

Fatigue was making a mess out of my unpacking as I sought to silently untangle my gear on a top bunk. There were three other hikers sleeping in close proximity, so I brought my rucksack out to the common room so as not to disturb them. Just as I was heading back to the bedroom there was a knock on the hostel door. The warden had gone home for the night, but feeling brave I opened it to the curious sight of a young man clutching a bike, his arm held by a policeman. The young guy, who was called José, was in cycling shorts, his arm was bleeding and his bike was damaged. My initial perception was that José was a prisoner being taken by the police into custody (we were in the old jail after all). The truth was less dramatic: José had arrived late into town and had asked the police for help. They brought him to the hostel and, being a little overly officious, insisted that that he should register and pay for a room.

I instinctively knew that I should get José inside fast so I helped him wheel in his old-style racing bike. Tiptoeing around the now almost full hostel, we got him a free bed. Back in the common room I began telling him about my police–prisoner misperception and we both began to laugh at the absurdity of it all. Soon, we were reduced to hysterical snorts and wheezes. Eventually we said goodnight and I wished him well on his goal to get to Santiago in five days. He reminded me a lot of Robert Powell from the film *Jesus of Nazareth*.

That night as I did my usual Review of the Day, I was struck by what an outstanding day it had turned into. There were so many good things, including the improving weather, the beauty of Comillas, meeting Miguel, the special Mass and procession, and finally encountering José. Most significant however, was how I hadn't let the Spanish woman get to me or ruin my day. With some help from Ignatius I was able to see the day through God's eyes: see the gift that it had been, even see the Spanish woman with compassion and reinterpret what could have been a toxic situation. Far from ruining my day it had focused me, energised my quest to do the Camino my way, and brought me all sorts of unexpected rewards – friends, community and significant experiences.

The warm feeling from the day before quickly evaporated as I arose washed out and haggard. I hadn't slept a wink due to the guy opposite me snoring loudly. He had roared and receded like waves on a pebble beach. I had tried a few tricks, including whistling and coughing loudly, but nothing worked. Tired and cranky, I found myself packing my things beside the snorer during the morning exodus. I found the anger within me ratcheting up to confront him when he turned and disarmed me with a smile. Completely oblivious to the nocturnal frustrations he had caused, he was bright as a button. Instead, I was the one who was still carrying the frustration. His infectious enthusiasm brightened up my day too.

I set off just after 6.00 a.m., first out of the hostel, wanting to be alone in nature. It was another lovely morning, the sky roseate, though it felt cool – ideal walking weather. I skirted some tidal estuaries first, the low water revealing the silty contours and fingers of the river basins. Then I wound my way up into the Cantabrian hills, which reflected shades of green, blue and grey. As I came down a narrow rutted track I met a grim-looking farmer with a sickle over his shoulder. Introducing himself as Francisco, he gave me an affable run-down on horses, feed, the harvest and fishing. I marvelled again at the way walking connected me to him and to the land through story.

I had already walked over 10 kilometres and was hungry. I didn't come across a café until I reached San Vincente, a lovely town built around a bay, accessible by a long stone causeway. As I sat outside a café, I spotted a familiar rickety bike and rider. I greeted José, the guy from the hostel the previous night. He joined me for coffee and we laughed again over the events of the night before. We began talking about our lives, and especially about philosophy, film and theories on life. Totally engaged, I forgot about being competitive or getting ahead on the Camino; this was much more important, the human connection. Spontaneous and flowing, we were living in the moment and being present to the other. This moment lived on in my memory as a 'hearts on fire'[78] experience. I was happy to find out subsequently that José did make it all the way to Santiago on his beat-up bike.

Later that day I bumped into my priest friend, Miguel, who was now in the company of a Frenchman, Lionel, and two young sisters from California, Liz and Virginia. Unaccustomed to walking with others, it took me a while to relax and see this as a gift too – the fun of walking as a group. I couldn't help noticing that Lionel was carrying a super slim daypack. Intrigued, I discovered he was on a 'Camino-plus' deal whereby his bag was carried for him, his lunches were pre-packed and he slept in pre-booked hotel rooms. This news took a bit of getting used to and yet it was an inevitable part of marketing that opened the Camino up to all types of walkers. I was glad that he was experiencing the Way anyhow, though glad too of my own freely chosen traditional 'pilgrim' method. Maybe I really was becoming less judgemental and more accepting.

We stopped for lunch at a country bar, chasing the chickens from the door as we entered. Lunch was a noisy affair with the television blaring behind us and the conversation animated by several beers. Having different nationalities present added to the conversation and the cultural differences were evident. For example, the American women treated the Camino like a holiday and Lionel wanted a relaxing hike, while for Miguel it was a serious pilgrimage. Afterwards we went our separate ways, the sisters returning home, and I was alone again. I breathed a sigh of relief back on the road; it had been delightful company but tough going for a solitary pilgrim.

Uncharacteristically, I found myself walking in the heat of the afternoon with new challenges. One was trekking through a working quarry layered in white sand, which created a blinding glare and was also tough going. Finally the trail led up a long concrete lane that ran almost vertically uphill and had me gasping. It was late afternoon when I arrived in Pesues, a village some 4 kilometres from my final destination. After trying a few side roads I could see no yellow arrows and realised I was lost. Retracing my steps I went back to the plaza and asked directions from a group of teenagers intensely playing Spanish guitar in a bus shelter. Graciously, they gave me directions. Aware of their considerable talent, I hung around as they resumed their singing. Genuinely interested, I applauded them to show my support and appreciation. I couldn't help mentioning that I too played guitar; immediately one young guy offered me his guitar. I played a U2 song, 'With or Without You', then passed the guitar back, and so we took turns playing different songs. Finally we hit on the ideal configuration – I would sing classic rock songs in English and the young guy would accompany me on guitar. We went through 'Sweet Home Alabama', 'Stairway to Heaven', 'Hotel California' and many others. Even though we barely spoke a word to each other, we had a glorious hour of sharing music and song. It was another memorable Camino moment, spontaneous and inclusive.

Dusk was falling as we finished and I began to look for accommodation. My two friends Miguel and Lionel appeared out of the gloom. It turned out that Lionel had a reservation in the two-star hotel on the main road and he invited us to stay there too. Done in as I was, I decided to take up the offer, though Miguel grumbled for a while before accepting. Safely tucked in bed I realised it had been another great day, full of adventure, connections and people. I was grateful; maybe I was getting the Camino 'thing'.

Soul Crisis

The Hotel Baviera in Pesues was not exactly plush; the rooms were more like tin boxes fitted out with iron furniture and linoleum. A grey dawn filtered through the metal shutters and consciousness arrived with a start. The doors around me rattled and banged as other guests, mainly hikers, performed their morning ablutions. Packing was easy with such scant belongings and like a refugee I had learned to leave everything ready for a quick exit. After a hurried wash I went downstairs for a meagre breakfast, joining Lionel and Miguel, my two friends from the day before. They wanted to set a tough pace and, sensing my reluctance, arranged a rendezvous later that night. I had a bad feeling about my increasingly painful right foot, and with relief watched them go.

Though I was hobbling somewhat, I was happy to be alone on the road again: that pilgrim magic. Looking somewhat like a camel, my washed clothes were pinned to my pack to dry, a trick I learned from the internet. I headed downhill on a broad multi-lane road towards the sleepy town of Unquera as the sun rose into a flawless azure sky. The town had arranged itself along the River Deva and was dominated by a hill on the north side. By the time I reached the outskirts of the town some forty minutes later I was limping, in considerable pain, and knew I was in trouble. The planned rendezvous with my friends wasn't going to happen. I was crestfallen; these recurring problems seemed insurmountable, a crushing dispiriting burden.

Frankly, I had been ignoring problems with this foot all along. My Dutch friend had drawn attention to this, and it explained all the blisters and pain. I suspected poor arch support in my shoes, a structural issue that, though hidden, was now becoming evident. Disconsolate, I wanted to give up, to throw myself to the ground and weep. I felt like such a failure, especially as this was the third such crisis. Maybe this trip was doomed or there was something fundamentally wrong with me. I felt the withering hand of worthlessness and despair on my shoulder. I had a sudden flash of insight into what Donal must have felt: the crushing burden of repeated failure, and the numbing bleakness of only seeing one way out. Remembering how this shadow gradually eclipsed my brother reminded me how easily darkness comes to dominate.

Ignatius of Loyola also had the experience of his life becoming unbearable, to the point of considering harming himself. I had been amazed to read that Ignatius, renowned saint and mystic, was once on the verge of suicide. As part of his transformation from courtier to pilgrim, he went through a harsh process of self-denial and fasting, recklessly adopting extreme penitential measures. His self-contempt and obsessive scruples were such that he considered throwing himself out a window in Manresa to end his mental anguish. Clearly in the grip of great depression, false perfectionism brought him to the verge of self-destruction. I had read an article by Ignatian scholar Joseph Munitiz, who argued that clinical depression was the overriding cause, and that Ignatius wasn't acting from spiritual desolation, which looks very similar.[79] Significantly, the extremes of depression and attempted suicide did force him to face reality (that he was on the point of starvation) and to act decisively against this damaging negativity (by abandoning excesses and banning scrupulosity). Additionally, he was able to spiritually discern that the disgust he was feeling about his new reformed lifestyle and the temptation to abandon it was the action of the bad spirit.[80] He experienced this as feelings of desolation, working to undo the progress he had made.

How I wished that Donal could have used this same reflective ability to avoid suicide. Obviously the whole issue of his depression was a mitigating factor and had clouded Donal's perception, as it had Ignatius'. However, Ignatius' spiritual insights would have been useful in recognising destructive impulses (e.g. isolation, stress) and distinguishing them from those that were genuinely life giving. Ignatius' whole system of reflection and discernment was precisely about making good decisions. During this inner turmoil we see Ignatius' process develop: reflecting on his emotions, judging which emotions are not genuinely good and then making life-affirming decisions (in his case, resuming eating, not harming himself). It is a profound but practical spirituality that all Jesuits learn. Sadly, I had tried to teach some of this discernment to my troubled brother but even fraternal bonds are not strong enough to deal with such powerful forces.

I was experiencing a similar emotional morass here in Unquera as I paced the riverbank. In refusing to accept the injury (avoiding reality) and by procrastinating I was undermining the reflective process. I was tempted to pack it all in and go home, or to walk on and ignore the foot pain, or even take some painkillers to make it go away. After a prolonged struggle, I felt some freedom and openness creep in about seeking help. I was praying to make the best decision, not to give in to an easy fix that could be costly in the long run. It made sense to take a detour to fix my foot, but I had a sense of failure and embarrassment about breaking off the Camino again. Imprisoned by guilt, I felt I was letting everyone down, including Donal. Was this actually a good basis for making a decision though? The strength of the conflicting emotions was paralyzing me. I thought of Ignatius lying on his sixteenth-century sickbed agonising over the broken leg that had put paid to his military career. Interestingly, he had found the answer within himself, being able to go deeper than his superficial feelings and arriving at a place of peace. He was to formulate this later as 'indifference'.[81] I needed some of this now.

In a flash of insight I decided that I would get the injury sorted out properly, regardless of my surface emotions and feelings. It galvanised me into action: I would go to the nearby city of Oviedo to get treatment and then rest for a while to allow my foot to heal. With time running out I had to get it right to be able to walk into Santiago. I studied Oviedo on the map, an hour away; it was a big city but located on yet another Camino route, the *Primitivo*. I rang my Jesuit friend José in Burgos and he organised my stay with the Jesuit community in Oviedo. Shortly it was all arranged and I was at peace again, having coffee and waiting for the bus.

I took a stroll along the Deva River and admired the terracotta-roofed townhouses opposite. The river was like glass, moving effortlessly by. Not for the first time, I wondered where this Camino was taking me. Taking a detour from the main Camino and being out of action for a while was hard medicine. I hoped to rejoin the walk soon, injury free and with renewed energy. I prayed to be open to what Oviedo would bring, that I would be well received and that I would get the necessary help. I really wanted to be restored to finish my quest in memory of Donal – the only thing that mattered.

Within a few minutes I was on the bus for Oviedo and sitting in air-conditioned luxury. I marvelled at how the distance of a whole day's walking could be effortlessly achieved in minutes; no wonder it felt like cheating! Out of habit I scoured the mountains looking for hikers but could see none. I appreciated every little thing, especially the spectacular scenery passing my window. I was now in another province, Asturias (having already walked through the Basque Country and Cantabria), and the imposing Picos de Europa were on my left. The rugged limestone and glaciated surfaces gave them an unreal quality, as if they could not possibly sustain such shapes. I read that there were bears and wolves there, so remote and extensive was the park. I intended to get some sleep but the thrilling view wouldn't allow it. 'This is an unexpected gift', I thought, warming up to this new adventure.

The bus pulled into Oviedo around noon and, out of habit, the first thing I did was make up a chorizo sandwich on a sunny park bench. Everything seemed charged with possibility in the dazzling sunlight. The Jesuit residence on Doctor Casal Street was so close that, despite my injury, I was able to walk there. Seeing this exotic city for the first time, the amalgam of traffic, plazas, cafés and apartments was intoxicating. Excited, I asked a man to take a photo of me. A very friendly guy, he told me he was from Cuba and only had temporary residence in Spain. We traded stories about how we had gotten here. I told him I would like to go to Cuba one day; we parted laughing. It seemed the Camino magic hadn't left me. On Doctor Casal Street the buildings were tall and imposing, mainly apartment blocks with a church on the corner. I wondered what the welcome would be.

To my relief, Brother José Manuel, who met me, was the epitome of hospitality. I was given a room on the sixth floor and took a moment to settle in. Not for the first time, I was so grateful for the Jesuit network and its ready hospitality across the world. At that stage I felt a great weariness but waited for lunch to meet the others in the community. They were relatively young and very welcoming, especially when they realised I had some Spanish. Afterwards, I had a much-needed siesta and then José Manuel brought me to the commercial district. It turned out that he was a self-styled expert in foot problems and knew exactly where to go. I marvelled at the serendipity of this. We went to an orthotic specialist who appeared to know José Manuel personally. She was very helpful, measured my feet and showed me various insoles, but she didn't have anything in my size. After much searching we finally found a chemist who had the right size. We left the shop triumphant, the new insoles fitted, and with a packet of anti-inflammatories just in case. Even my foot seemed to feel better already. I felt indebted to José Manuel for his persistence and constant generosity to me, a virtual stranger.

After a dinner of monkfish, vegetables and sliced potatoes, one of the Jesuit priests invited me to evening Mass at the nearby Sacred Heart Church. The church façade was made of white limestone and red brick. Inside it had a strong community feel to it and was packed out. It was the feast of the Sacred Heart of Jesus,[82] which meant a glorious combination of Mass, the rosary, recital of the novena prayer and then exposition after Mass. Seeing the sea of faces bowed in adoration, I was struck by the variety of different paths to God; I had been finding God in the erratic nature of the road, while here an ancient devotion was celebrated. I felt so deeply grateful for all that the Camino had given me; I knew personally of God's providence and protective care. With rising emotion I felt that Donal, no matter the tragedy of his life and death, could never be outside this encompassing love of the Sacred Heart.[83] I felt heartened on my mission, temporarily stalled, by this insight.

Returning home a huge party was in full swing in the city. One could be forgiven for thinking that the Spanish have one fiesta after another given my experience in the last few days. Seeing the fireworks from the rooftop that night, I instinctively reviewed the highlights of the day. I had much to be grateful for: essentially I had received food and shelter, I had some great Jesuit companions around me, and to top it off it looked as though my foot problem had been solved, all in one fell swoop. Could it be that this new start was the end of all my walking problems? The Camino was temporarily suspended as I recuperated from its ravages in this safe house.

I sank into bed for some long overdue rest. Unconsciousness reigned … but suddenly something had a grip on me and I felt the panic rise. I was trapped, pinned to the bed and couldn't get free no matter how hard I tried. Frightened, I struggled even harder to no avail. With a shock I realised that I was almost totally paralyzed, it was creeping through my organs and I was slowly dying. I toyed with giving into it, sliding into oblivion, but something held me back. 'I'm not ready to die, I want to live', was my urgent thought. I thrashed and raged at the hidden chains. Suddenly consciousness raced in, and I woke up in a sweat from the dream's grip. It took me some moments to work out where I was, and gradually I came to a sitting position on the bed.

The morning sun struggled to enter the double layer of curtain and blinds, rendering the sunlight a murky brown. I was in Oviedo, in the ancient kingdom of Asturias, and I was alive. I came to with some incredulity, remembering the eventful last few days. Miraculously, I was still on the Camino and relatively intact, in spite of the events that had conspired to throw me off course. The kindness of the community here had saved me in many different ways, especially in getting my foot problem sorted and giving me a shot at getting to Santiago. Gratitude overcame me like a warm glow. I had been given yet another chance when all had seemed lost.

I had the luxury of a day off and time to reflect, of which I felt Ignatius would have approved.[84] There was also a beautiful city to explore. I found the Gothic Cathedral of San Salvador impressive but it was the Cámara Santa, an interior treasure room, which was intriguing. It contained the Shroud of Oviedo, the bloodstained cloth that reputedly wrapped the head of Christ in the tomb. It was a symbol for suffering and transition; 'the cost of love', I thought.

I mused about my own life as a series of little deaths and new beginnings, whether it was changing career, joining the Jesuits, going to a new country (Colombia, Canada), or hard-won learnings and insights. The hardest thing I had ever faced, however, was scraping myself back together after the devastating loss of Donal to suicide. Suicide had totally reconfigured everything for me: relationships, sureties, view of the world, faith, the very ground where I stood. The grief process after suicide was terrifying, unlike any other. There was a shocking brutality to the manner of his death. I was left with all these unanswered questions – the persistent 'why' question and 'what did I do wrong?' among others. I felt I had failed Donal in not being vigilant enough and had missed some key warning signs. The result was insidious burdens of guilt and remorse. I tried to stagger on as normal but it seemed increasingly impossible to cope under the crushing weight. Only reaching the limit of my abilities and coping strategies brought about change. It forced me to reach beyond my comfort zone, beyond even the normal supports of friends and of counselling. Ironically, it was my belief in the spiritual, recast in the fire of suffering, that was key to providing meaning and support in this darkest of processes.

I obsessed about Jesus' moment on the cross where he faces awful agony and feels that God, his father, has abandoned him.[85] From within my own suffering I felt the same sense of desertion. For Jesus, the absence of pleasant feelings or comforting presence didn't mean God was absent to him. I had to face up to this paradoxical truth too. It was cold comfort but Ignatius of Loyola would have agreed with this also. It's not superficial *feelings* that are important in staying the course but managing to persevere as Jesus did through the pain. As a Jesuit, it was a tough challenge blindly hanging on, a broken heart in search of healing.

Applying the Jesuit catchphrase 'finding God in all things' seemed both repulsive and intriguing when facing a suicide. For the longest time I held God to blame, an easy target for my anger. I had this persistent dream-like image where I held my brother's body in my arms up to God and howled

in anger and recrimination. There was no answer. Was it
God not caring or his inability to act? It did, however, expose
some of my naïve beliefs: that God would protect me from
bad things, and that God was responsible for everything that
occurred.[86] Before I could let God off the hook though, I had
to pass through the purifying furnace of grief. It was a blind
roller-coaster ride, guaranteed to expel false pride and self-
reliance. Who was I to question God or hold God accountable?
The process helped with the reshaping of my faith, bringing about a new understanding. Central to it was humility
and gratitude, seeing everything as a gift. Unfortunately, it
nearly took my mind too, the ravages of soul pain exacting a
terrible cost. I knew early on I had to get help.

A few years ago something impelled[87] me to seek a support
group and initially I joined a depression group by mistake.
Eventually they steered me towards a suicide bereavement
group, Console,[88] which was to become my home. Initially
my anxiety was high – would I be judged for what happened to Donal? Would I be labelled too or seen to be at risk?
Committed to find some support, I joined a small group of
fairly normal-looking people in north Dublin one blustery
autumn evening. The head of the organisation, Paul Kelly,
spoke courageously about losing his sister, Sharon, and why
he had set up Console. It gave me courage and like the others
I slowly found my voice over the next few weeks.

The stories people unleashed were savage and excruciating.
There were tears and regrets and immeasurable heartache.
Like ships in an unmerciful storm we were all dashed onto
the rocks of ubiquitous grief. We couldn't save anyone from
their situation, but the bonds of solidarity were such that
we could survive the worst ravages together. Just knowing there was someone listening, who would listen without
judgement, was an anchor. I came away from those meet-
ings reeling from the onslaught of tragedy but paradoxically
renewed to have witnessed such transparency. Most encour-
aging was realising there was a profound healing process

that eventually buoyed everyone to the surface, a self-righting mechanism. Over time I could see people shift and move, often not fully healed but managing to get by. Maybe God was in this after all, but not in the way I expected.[89]

My day off in Oviedo had revealed much more than I bargained for, yet it sharply defined the quest I was on and the answers I sought. It was more clearly a grief journey; I became conscious of the burden I carried and for which I sought relief. I longed for the open road once more.

The Road of Kings

I was having a crisis of identity, a hiker on a day off from the trail. The Camino was so all-consuming that taking time off felt like cheating. Yet here I was in Oviedo, in northwest Spain, holed up in an apartment away from my originally planned route and significantly behind on my itinerary. Far from the frantic hurry of *peregrinos* (pilgrims), I was relaxing and resting my tired legs and muscles, fortified by my new insoles. Yet somehow I couldn't enjoy it very much; rather I felt uneasy and slightly guilty. On the one hand, my body was telling me that I needed rest to heal and recuperate, but my mind was strident: 'You're off track, this is wasted time; you will surely pay for this.' Of course there was some value in keeping on schedule, but I had to reflect more to discover what was important.

Trying to keep to the original plan did not seem to be wise based on the injuries I had suffered. There is an element of being stretched on the Camino of course, but I suspected that I was ignoring my body's wisdom and that I was forcing my body at too hard a pace. This is a very individual thing of course, which everyone has to judge for themselves by listening to their body. I knew many people on the Camino learn this lesson the hard way, injuring themselves, being unable to continue and having to return home prematurely.[90] My hunch was that, like me, people were allowing the head to dominate the body and suffering the consequences.

Ignatius of Loyola had some hard-won expertise in this area. He himself did great damage to his health with excessive fasts, prolonged pilgrimages and scant regard for his body. He walked some incredible distances on foot, crisscrossing Europe, the prototypical poor pilgrim begging his way through Spain, France and Italy. Originally thinking that he was doing all these great ascetical deeds for God, he slowly came to the realisation that it was the excessive element that was damaging and was often neither helpful nor from God. Sometimes these penances were beneficial, but only up to a point. Gradually he discovered that he was called to a more balanced approach with regard to walking, fasting and eating.

The insight he eventually came to was captured by the ingenious phrase 'insofar as' (*tanto cuanto* in Spanish),[91] meaning that anything can be helpful and a way to God *insofar as* it genuinely does come from God and deepens one's humanity. This means examining decisions to see where they come from and lead towards, to see if they really are good (from God), or if they are coming from the ego, from rigidity or from negativity, even self-hate. For example, my initial decision to walk over 25 kilometres a day on the Camino was proving to be a painfully unrealistic goal, and in need of some adjustment. I needed to let go of some destructive ideas in my head (the perfect walk) and adjust to the actual reality of my situation: frequent injuries, a reduced fitness level, and the need for more recuperation and rest. Surprisingly, taking it easy in the Jesuit apartment felt like a wise option in that it would directly help me with the goal of getting to Santiago. I felt the word stir my heart, the finishing line almost within reach.

The Jesuit community in Oviedo had given me a great welcome and made me feel very much at home. They understood the Camino well, several of the younger members having walked it. As the itinerant 'pilgrim' guest, I really appreciated the atmosphere of trust and affection, which means a lot when you are away from home. I enjoyed an informal Asturian dinner that night: crab stew, salmon, blue cheese and a local wine. We squeezed around a circular table, with a solitary light suspended over it, and lingered on after the meal enjoying the fun. Like the Irish there was a bit of *tomando el pelo* (leg-pulling), and I was delighted to find that my Spanish allowed me to join in.

Strangely, I had a strong sense of Donal's presence at the table that night. He always loved being at the centre of the fun and his easy sense of humour attracted people to him. I found myself taking on the same role, remembering the best parts of him. This was a real gift to me, allowing for some much-needed levity to offset the grim elements of my quest. In a small way, I felt he was helping me put aside the burden of grief that night and I benefited from this light-hearted escapism. Taking on one of his best attributes made him present, and I felt that I and everyone there was the better for it. This last night in Oviedo was poignant, as the beckoning Camino was calling. Providentially, Oviedo was at the start of another route, the *Camino Primitivo*, which would bring me directly to Santiago.

The next morning I woke feeling lousy, a pulsating headache wanting to bury me in the bed. Nursing my sore head, I groaned as I sat up, remembering that I had gone out cider-tasting the previous night. It seemed like such a great idea the night before when one of the Jesuits, Fermín, invited me to a *sidería* (cider house) with some prayer group friends. I thought I would make my apologies and go to bed early, but I got carried away in a passionate conversation about the Northern Ireland peace process. The captivating party piece in the *sidería* was the waiter pouring cider from above his head into a glass at knee height. The cider was so aerated as a result that it felt like champagne. 'Why did I not stop after one glass?' I berated myself. I was feeling dreadful now though;

my whole body felt like taking a sick day. I forced myself out of the house and staggered onto the street, remembering Ignatius' rule of thumb about sticking to a previously made decision.[92] I had my new insoles and socks on for courage; I was ready to begin again, though hampered by a fierce headache and dehydration.

Legend has it that King Alfonso II had a vision of stars impelling him to walk this new Camino. I was operating from slightly less romantic principles that day. Alfonso II had constructed a church, San Julián de los Prados, in the ninth century on the outskirts of the city and I chose that as my official starting point. A UNESCO World Heritage Site, it was over 1,000 years old but the ochre, crimson and yellow frescos were still startling to my bleary eyes. The effect was that of being enclosed in a red velvet picture book. Alfonso II was the great defender of Asturias and also apparently the first pilgrim to walk to Santiago de Compostela, and the one who built the cathedral there over the remains of the Apostle James. He had created this *Camino Primitivo* (the 'original' or 'first road'), the classic route, which I would now be walking into Santiago. 'This was where it all began,' I thought, 'in the footsteps of kings, nobles and pilgrims.'

On the *Camino Primitivo* proper, once I had cleared the suburbs I started to feel a bit more human and slightly regal as the hangover wore off. I felt regret at leaving my original *Camino del Norte*, but I needed this direct mountain route to get me to Santiago on time. Again, I felt like I was beginning a new chapter, as if all the previous walking was just a preparation. As with every change, there were pros and cons: this route was much busier with less solitude, but much better served with signs and hostels. The guidebook indicated there would be huge mountains and some intimidating rocky passes. Here, however, the Camino looked every inch the medieval royal way: it was cut deeply into the earth, paved with cobbles and meandered through fields with curves very pleasing to the eye.

Alone and on foot – Early morning in Asturias

Queuing for the hostel in Markina

Confusing signpost in the Basque country

The challenging ascent from Pasajes de San Juan

The spectacular cathedral at Burgos

The Camino markers in the Basque country

Santa Juliana procession in Santillana del Mar

Camino coastal walk near Santander

Lezama church holy water font

Sunrise near Castro-Urdiales, my second start

In the festival procession at Comillas: the parish priest, Miguel and me

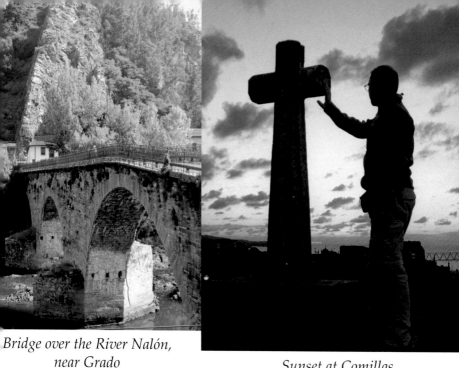

*Bridge over the River Nalón,
near Grado*

Sunset at Comillas

One of the many variations on the Camino markers

80-year-old Anton, me and Frederick outside Tineo

The Cantabrian mountains near Pola de Allande, the infamous 'Roof of the Camino'

Larking around with the Mexican Alvarez family (I'm dressed as St James)

On arriving in Santiago Cathedral

Santiago Cathedral – front façade

Where the Camino meets the se
Finisterre (Kilometre 0)

The place of 'the burning', Cape Finisterre

Once out of Oviedo it was refreshing to see the iconic *flechas amarillas* again and soon I was striding out among fields, livestock and the busyness of farming. The undulating meadows, grassland and chugging tractors reminded me of my home county of Fermanagh, renowned for its 'basket of eggs' glaciated landscape and its rich pastoral tapestry. There was something about being in the country that was refreshing and renewing; it lifted the heart and opened the soul to God. Now that my morning fug had worn off, I was elated to be on the road again, without encumbrance. My attention turned outward, freed from the hangover's internal pain. The sight of a familiar red Massey Ferguson tractor in a shed lifted my soul, reminding me of carefree summers of our family childhood on the farm before 'the great sadness'.[93] I had a memory of hay bales and tractor races with my brothers, a paradise of innocence before the storm. Memory restored my faith; all was well in the world. It was invigorating to be walking earthy country lanes, seeing the mountains, feeling alive. Surely nothing could stop me now?

There was one difference I noticed however.[94] I was going at my own pace, stopping when I felt like it, not rushing and taking time to drink in the rural vista. I felt like I was finally learning to slow down and 'smell the flowers'. My hard-won experiential learning invited me to be in the present moment, to let go of agendas and expectations. I felt I was present to myself and to everything around me. I internalised this 'mindfulness'[95] resolve by only doing 10 kilometres on my first day back on the road. What I had assimilated from the last few weeks' experience was not pushing my limits, listening to my body and being aware of the experience.[96] As a result, the world seemed to sparkle with possibility, my perception was bright and clear, and I lived a deep sense of consolation and connectedness to God, present in the world. Could it be that I had made progress?

Despite taking my time and getting lost once, I got to the nondescript brick *albergue* fairly quickly. On the outskirts of a village, it was surrounded by fields. As it was around noon and I still had some hours until it opened, I went back to the bar I had passed along the road and had the cheap *menu del día* meal. I relished in taking my time eating and in enjoying the food, my new philosophy. I also met some other pilgrims there who were trying to persuade me to walk on further. Avoiding the temptation, I let them go, unconcerned about what they thought. Then I went back to the locked hostel and found some sleeping mats and had a cool improvised siesta in its shady porch. Afterwards, feeling bored and wandering around the area, I came across an elderly woman seated outside her apartment with crutches beside her. Her face was kindly and lined, but collapsed on one side. She explained that she had had a stroke and that her mobility was reduced as a result. Her story relativised my own fairly minor complaints. A model of kindness, she told me that I could get a key for the hostel back in the same bar.

I walked back to the bar for the key, avoiding the trap of frustration at all the back and forth. Letting myself into the hostel, it was pretty dirty at first sight. It obviously hadn't been cleaned since the previous night, but on the upside it was bright and airy. The other pilgrims started to arrive en masse: several Dutch people; a Spaniard; and a Frenchman, Anton, who was 80 years old (a former marathon runner I discovered), and his Belgian companion Frederick. I was thrilled to recognise a Dutch woman, Anuk, one of the original group I had met in my first week. Introductions were made and we were quickly a community of pilgrims, cooperating to help everyone settle in and feel welcome.

After the flurry of showers and clothes washing, there was a long mellow session lounging on the balcony in the evening sun talking about hostels, stages and guidebooks – all that good pilgrim stuff. Sunset found us all sitting around the dinner table on the terrace at the nearby bar. The food – the staple steak and chips – was very agreeable, leaving us relaxed and content. From our elevated outside terrace looking over a dusky valley, a blazing sunset dazzled our eyes. This day had brought good companions, got me back on route and reenergised my mission. Tearful behind my sunglasses, I thought to myself, 'This is such an amazing life, I am so grateful for all this day brought; thank God I was able to get out of bed this morning and not miss this.' Thanks to Ignatius too for his useful rule of thumb.

At dawn, a misty turquoise sunrise drew me out of bed early to stand in a stubbly field in contemplation.[97] Used to being the first one on the road, this time I let the others pass me as I took in the beauty. I felt God was communicating with me through this dawn. I felt I was being invited to begin the day with gratitude and let the rest be.

I felt something shift within me; I was seeing the world born anew, made of light and dew. The country lane was a little piece of heaven, made of fields, lanes and hedgerows with all their attendant smells, sights and sounds. Some sheep bleated out their staccato accompaniment. I hardly noticed the time[98] go by, held in the moment. I only reluctantly stopped for *café con leche* to get some much-needed sustenance. All the other pilgrims had gone ahead of me now. I let them go, content to walk my own Camino.

Later I fell in with a Belgian pair: a father who had walked over 2,000 kilometres, literally from his front door, and his son, who had joined him in Oviedo, the plan being to finish the Camino together. However, the father was vastly fitter, all tanned muscles and technique, while the son was lagging behind, his legs still white and muscles soft. I said goodbye; they were going too fast for me. As they walked off into the early mist I had a sense of foreboding – the disparity between them seemed too great and the distance between them irreconcilable. I was to meet the son ten days later, his feet too damaged to walk. He was zoned out watching television, hell-bent on escapism as he despondently made arrangements to head home. I held them in my heart, their good desire for time together having been overcome by condition and circumstance.

By noon I had made it into a large country town, Grado, where I managed to get a welcome lunch and a wifi connection for checking my email. Setting off again, I could feel the heat build, especially climbing a steep rocky hill en route to the next village, El Fresno. This was only a taste of the famed Cantabrian Mountains, my last great barrier before Santiago. I tried not to think about what lay ahead.

As I stopped for a rest at a crossroads, a young couple were shelling runner beans beside me, so focused on their task they didn't notice me for some moments. I asked for directions, and they told me that there was a hostel up ahead, near the top of the next huge hill. Weighing things up, I decided that I could climb it if I had a siesta first, and so went into a newly cut hayfield and lay down for twenty minutes. Outdoor snoozes reveal a captivating view of the sky and clouds, notwithstanding the nefarious insect bites.

Refreshed, I laboured up the hill in low gear, gasping at times. By the time I reached the top my stomach was growling and I ate some more peanuts and fruit from my bag. Though I found a welcome water fountain, I could see no sign of a hostel. I had no choice then but to continue over the top and downhill. It was even steeper and more treacherous, a mix of rock and blue clay, and very hard on the legs. I was glad it wasn't wet or slippery though; a fall would have been all I needed. When I arrived in the next village, still I could find no hostel or bar. The first couple must have misdirected me, or I had misunderstood. There was no point in getting mad about it, so I merely put the best interpretation on it,[99] believing they genuinely wanted to help me. I chalked it up and let it go; there was no point in worrying about it. However, it meant I had to walk several kilometres to the next hamlet, Escamplero. My feet were hurting at this stage as I struggled to stay positive.

Desperate to avoid any more walking, I went into the only bar in town, not holding out much hope of a bed. Incredibly, when I asked, they offered a bed in their tiny *albergue* out the back. I laughed to see it was actually a wooden garden shed, with only four beds, the smallest hostel I had seen. I was, however, exceedingly grateful to lay down my pack and relax. Inside, there was a bitter rank smell of creosote but it felt like a palace through the glaze of my fatigue. I had some supper in the bar with a German couple who were vegetarians (unfortunately by the time I discovered this I had already ordered a meal of chorizo and bacon), and who spoke excellent English. They were doing a holiday on the Camino, looking for the most scenic parts, and were planning on doubling back to the coast again. I told them I was an Irish priest on the Camino, but didn't tell them of my rather personal quest. We passed a very pleasant meal together and my good humour came flooding back with food and rest.

Later, as I unpacked my bag another hiker arrived in the shed-hostel, Pedro, a stocky, swarthy Spaniard. With such small quarters I was wondering how we would get on, but thankfully we hit it off right away. Within half an hour, we were sitting outside like kings on the flimsy garden furniture, having a beer together. We talked at length about schools as we were both teachers. Inevitably, the conversation turned to the allure of the Camino, and he told me he was doing it for the fifth time, a stage every year. Evening was falling and likewise the temperature. We noticed the loud roaring of the calves in the field right next to us. I explained to him about weaning, where the calf and cow are separated in the first year and how the noise of the calf crying for its mother would last all night. It was a bizarre and surreal nightfall; in a garden shed at the back of a bar, accompanied by a calf chorus. This day had brought some great things – I had to let go of a certain amount, but it ended well; I knew I was back in Camino mode.

Alone and on Foot

My new friend, Pedro, and I were up at 6 a.m. to witness a grey, overcast morning, perfect for walking. Within minutes we had packed everything in our shoebox of a room and were kitted out ready for the road. We left some Euros on the bed as this hostel invited a voluntary contribution. The weaned calves that had kept us awake half the night were now grazing, quiet and innocent as lambs. Swinging on our packs, we took the cobbled road to Cornellana, zipping up our jackets against the cold. I could see right away that Pedro was setting a stiff pace – he had only a week off and was determined to make the most of it. I wondered how long I could keep up; I decided I would stop when the going got too tough for me.

The path wound its way across several bridges over the Narcea River, famous for its salmon fishing, and Pedro pointed out the fishing spots along the way. The river itself was intriguing: a mottled mix of shade and light, currents and eddies, smooth and rough water. A metaphor for life itself, it tumbled and transformed, the essence of fluid motion, seeking a path around obstacles. The Atlantic salmon had made their way from the sea for centuries, running all sorts of gauntlets to spawn here, only to die soon after. I could picture the medieval stockades and barriers (*postas*) that were used to trap the fish; maybe pilgrims availed of the bounty at this very spot. It reminded me that I was engaged in my own uphill battle and would need some of the courage of wild salmon and the fluidity of water.

There was an eleventh-century Romanesque monastery called San Salvador on the outskirts of Cornellana that I really wanted to see, especially as there was an *albergue* housed within its walls. Having seen *The Way*[100] movie, I had romantic visions of pilgrims sleeping right in the cloisters with cowled monks gliding by in silent meditation. I also wanted to catch up with my original walking companions whom I missed so much. The monastery, however, was a terrible letdown, nothing like what I was expecting. Part of the inner courtyard had been turned into a pilgrim hostel but the rest was in a terrible state of disrepair. The façade was stained with storm water and the building bulged as if it would burst apart. This piece of rich ecclesial patrimony, built almost a thousand years ago, was falling into ruin. Also, there were no recognisable faces among the departing pilgrims.

The place distressed me greatly; something about that crumbling ruin reminded me of Donal's slide into despair. Like a building, he had slowly decayed over the years. I left at a run, Pedro following, anxious to get back to some of the natural beauty that the Camino excelled in. I later read in the local paper that there was a plan to renovate this once great building, so at least there was some hope. I put it out of my mind. In the town I stopped for the ubiquitous *café con leche y napolitana* (I had just discovered the *napolitana*, a puff pastry with a chocolate filling, which, though sugary, was a taste sensation) in a café, and regrettably said goodbye to the fast-walking Pedro. I felt a great fondness for his brusque friendship and gave thanks for the precious time we had spent together. In classic Camino fashion he was gone in an instant, and I knew we would not meet again, at least in this life.

Unwittingly, I took the wrong road out of town and found myself some 2 kilometres off course. Stubbornly refusing to retrace my steps, I took the advice of some locals to cut straight across country to re-join the Camino. The only trouble was that I had to climb through a quarry up a steep hill. Energy-wise, it was a costly short cut. Cresting the next hill however, an upland meadow rolled out before me littered with big, round, golden bales. The smell of sweet harvest hay hit me first, bringing me right back to those halcyon childhood days helping my father mow the fields. A bodily memory of wholeness settled upon me, a memory of life before the grimy rains of grief and loss had sullied it. Rejuvenated, I toiled on alone for many kilometres, managing to temporarily forget my burdens, happy just to be alive and moving. I reflected on what a gift each day, each moment, was – this richness continually on offer if one has the eyes for it.

I was reminded of Ignatius of Loyola and his journeys crisscrossing Europe, all on foot and largely alone. He was the prototypical pilgrim and the source of much of my inspiration as a Jesuit. I had left my career in computers to follow this pilgrim dream. Just as with the Camino, that meant being out 'on the road', exposed to whatever ups or downs this brought but also learning to trust in God's providence and care. Ignatius had learned over time the value of letting go and handing over. Now here I was searching for God and for answers on the Camino, where providence was paramount.

The Spanish phrase '*solo y a pie*' (alone and on foot) is closely associated with Ignatius of Loyola as it captures the key movements and journeys of his life. Here, on the Camino, I could relate to Ignatius' state of being in motion, open and trusting, as being tangibly close to God. On the road, I had come to understand that God is a pilgrim too, actively in search of me rather than being static, confined or rigid. I always liked the definition of God as a verb,[101] proactively engaging me in a divine dance,[102] a thrilling and often scary relationship. On the Camino I had been strongly challenged to let go of my burden, to find God in the immediate experience and to open up to real friendship and connection with others. I regularly felt that I was being called out of myself, opened up like a budding flower. I had a spring in my step and felt some real joy, an unfamiliar emotion since Donal's death.

Donal had been a great believer in providence, but almost as some kind of safety net that would catch him at the last moment. Like most brothers we fiercely debated every sort of topic between us, and none more so than religion. He was a great defender of the poor and outcast, identifying with them very strongly. His belief in a God who loves and cares for all people, no matter how downtrodden, was impressive. He would often put himself out for those in trouble, with no regard for his personal well-being or safety. He would often glorify destitution and chaos a little bit too much for my liking, as if we had no responsibility at all. I found myself thinking about the manner of his death a lot. Did he believe that God would save him from himself in that last awful self-destruction? I wondered what kind of a God he found there in that moment and whether he got the deep peace he was looking for. Nonetheless, I believed firmly that a loving God would understand the desperation of that blackest of moments.

Here it was the perfect morning; the sun shone hazily through the leafy canopy and a stream looped forward and backwards through a series of bridges on the track. As if to confirm this upbeat turn, I met a delightful Spanish grandfather and granddaughter on a stone bridge over a brook, his face lit by a serene smile. They were sauntering along, taking their time and enjoying the day, a model of being present and happy. Exchanging a few words with them, their joy was infectious and I left them lifted by the conversation. Then the valley opened up into a wide floodplain and was divided into rectangular strips of agricultural farmland alternating maize, spelt, beans and potatoes. The path was now exposed and the sun beat down more fiercely; I longed for some shade.

About noon I arrived into Salas, the principal town in the region, sweaty and hungry. Known at the 'Gateway to the West' for its strategic location in the mountains, the main street was dominated by the town's medieval tower and impressive Palacio Valdés. On a sugar low, all I could think about was getting calories and fluids fast. It was only then that I would appreciate my medieval and Roman surroundings. Reluctantly, I was just about to leave town when I saw a familiar blue and white T-shirt coming up the street. I was overjoyed to see Anuk, my Dutch friend whom I hadn't seen for some days. She was in bad shape, however, totally spent in a stupor of fatigue and defeat. I was shocked at how much weight she had lost; she was pencil thin, gaunt and worn. I bought her a coffee, surprised at how unresponsive she was. Intuiting that she needed some support, I reminded her of the huge journey that she had already made from Holland and how close she was to finishing and making it home. To my amazement, on hearing these words she sprung right up out of the chair and back onto the Camino without as much as a goodbye. I let her go, having become accustomed to respecting people's rhythms and privacy.

I bought some food supplies and headed up the steep hill out of town just as the sun was descending on its daily arc. Once more I was alone and on foot. On the edge of town a woman in an apron wished me 'Buen Camino' and also 'Go in peace', which really struck me, as it was almost biblical.[103] Within minutes, I was relieved to be in the shade, walking up a steep stony path that was carved precariously into the side of a ravine. On the right the path fell away steeply into a fast-flowing stream and, bizarrely, a four-lane highway hung suspended in the sky above me, seemingly from invisible supports. Mercifully, no traffic sounds broke the silence of nature. The heat was steadily building. Only a few minutes into the steep uphill climb I felt a stabbing pain in my left Achilles tendon. Trying to walk through the pain, my leg started to seize up like a rusty wheel, allowing less and less movement.

Overheated, frustrated and fed up, I threw a private tantrum: 'Why does this keep happening?! That's it, I've had it with this trip, I'm so sick of being injured, I'm finished.' Railing against the unfairness, I impetuously considered pushing on through the pain, driven on by thoughts of my friends ensconced in a cosy hostel at the top of the hill. I had to force myself to let those distractions go, to focus on the present moment and my immediate predicament. Even though my head was generating many seductive reasons to keep going, my body was telling me a greater truth. Made wiser through my previous Camino experiences of injury, I decided to stop. Gradually, calm returned to my agitated being and I cooled down.

As usual, there was no one around to help. I took some anti-inflammatories and did some self-help – stretching and massage – but it didn't seem to make much difference. Then I tried to sleep it off by taking a siesta at the side of the track, staying close to the wall of the steep ravine. Afterwards, I felt somewhat refreshed and gingerly began again the steep ascent along the river. Within two minutes the pain ripped through my tendon again. I had to face reality and reluctantly decided to call it a day and return to Salas. As I hobbled past the same woman with the apron again, she asked why was I going the wrong way on the Camino. And then, to my joy, I met again the 80-year-old Anton, officially the oldest person on the Camino that year, and his Belgian friend Frederick, who was accompanying him. I knew them well at this point and we exchanged some news of our adventures. They shared some water with me as I had run out and I shared some chocolate with them. Finally, I waved a fond farewell to them as they disappeared up the hill.

Back in town at yet another crossroads, I asked myself, 'Where do I get help?' I remembered the advice from Ignatius not to panic, but to trust in providence. Some solution would turn up eventually, though it seemed unlikely to me at that particular juncture, a stranger in a strange town. Negativity gnawed at me, planting the suspicion that I was probably finished on this Camino adventure. Then suddenly, I remembered that I had seen a physiotherapist's office on the hot march into town. This memory came back to me just when I needed it, and I got to the office before it closed. To my surprise, the physiotherapist, Davíd Fernandez, took me into his office right away. Even though there were a few other patients around he acted as if I (a sweaty, limping pilgrim) was the most important person in the world. He had me lie down and massaged both my calves, right into the bone, which was excruciatingly painful. He promised me a full recovery by the next day, which I found hard to believe, as I was in even more pain and hardly able to hobble.

He bid me a warm farewell, insisting that I immerse my leg in a cold bath that night ('Have you seen a hostel with a bath?' I wanted to ask him.) As we talked, I had the impression of a very competent and earnest young man, who was intelligent and aware, and who was slightly out of place in this provincial backwater. I imagined him with plans for a big city lifestyle, far from Salas. He astounded me by only charging €10 for the one-hour consultation. Once again, the kindness and care of virtual strangers was staggering. I presumed that having injured pilgrims turning up at his door was a regular occurrence but he never gave any hint of this. However, I was to be even more grateful to him the next day on the trail.

Limping past a fancy hotel, the Castillo de Valdés, built within a medieval castle, I saw to my amazement that the pilgrim *menu del día* was advertised. I was in like a shot, though I felt a bit out of place in their cool leafy courtyard, surrounded by tables dressed with starched linen. Regardless of my dusty, stained trail wear, I was treated royally. As soon as I tasted the velvety smoothness of the Rioja wine, I knew this was going to be something special. The starter was *emberzao*, a kind of a pork black pudding wrapped in cabbage leaves. This was followed by *fabada*, Asturian stew made of beans, pork sausage and bacon. Desert was my favourite, *arroz con leche y frixuelos*, a crêpe with rice pudding. It was probably due to the tough day I had had, but I was appreciative of every single morsel. I made a fool of myself by lavishing praise on each course to the waitress – I never enjoyed a meal so much. She must have wondered what poor food I had been eating up to now. Again, I felt it was providence that brought me such a culinary gift when I needed it most.

Fortified greatly by the wine, I got myself a room in the same hotel, justifying it in terms of the bath necessary to treat my leg. Walking into my luxurious room was overwhelming after grubby hostel living. The colours and velvety fabrics were so dazzling and unfamiliar I hardly dared touch them. In contrast, my meagre belongings seemed incongruous in this plush setting. I felt the wonder of a child exploring the room, the view and the historic parts of the hotel. I did feel somewhat ridiculous later though, shivering in the cold bath, thinking 'This Camino will be the end of me!'

Afterwards, feeling refreshed, I rushed out to try to get to Mass in the nearby sixteenth-century collegiate church, but to my dismay the priest was just finishing. I went up to talk to him afterwards and he introduced himself as Padre Adán, a friendly young man, who was pastor for a number of churches nearby. I explained who I was and what I was doing and to my joy he said he would be delighted to facilitate me celebrating Mass there and then. He generously offered to be my server and this really touched me. Whether it was the solemn air of the empty church or the novelty of the words in Spanish, I heard them as if for the first time:

Te damos gracias, Señor y Padre nuestro, te bendecimos y te glorificamos, porque has creado todas las cosas y nos has llamado a la vida.

We give you thanks Lord and Father, we bless you and glorify you, because you have created everything and called us into life.

The words spoke to my heart: I was grateful for all that I had received this particularly full day on the Camino. I certainly felt that it was a call to life and to rediscover something lost. Mostly however, I was overwhelmed with emotion and choked up on the Eucharist.[104] I don't know what poor Padre Adán thought of this sentimental Irishman but for me the import and meaning of this day was caught up in the rite, making it difficult to finish this most intimate celebration. To top it all off, Padre Adán went to his car and brought me a bag of *pan dulce* (sweetbread), which was to last me several days. I found all this hospitality a bit too much, this overwhelming generosity of strangers.

Just as the physiotherapist promised, my leg was as good as new the next day. I began again on that long, winding road uphill. Fortified by all the necessary food for the journey and all the support, I arrived in the cold and windy hilltop town of Tineo without event.

Desolation Road

A sharp sound fractured my unconsciousness and I awoke with a jolt. Though the hostel was a warm refuge from the mountain air, it had been a noisy place the previous night with almost every bed taken. Initially there was a lot of rustling and creaking as the forty-odd people settled down for the night. At 2 a.m. one couple dragged their mattresses out to sleep beside the toilets, and another pair rose at 5 a.m. to get on the road early. It was the departure of a large Spanish group accompanied by lots of torch flashes, ripping of Velcro fasteners and whispered conversations that woke me. I pulled the nylon pillow around my ears but I couldn't block it out. Never good in the morning, my nerves seemed particularly fractious that day. I had a bad feeling about the day ahead.

Bleary-eyed and drained, I forced myself up. Grabbing my backpack, I almost tripped over the couple sleeping beside the toilets. Once outside, the dark slowly dissolved and as I traversed the valley the sun traced its trajectory skywards. There were mountains everywhere, as far as the eye could see, a 'terrible beauty'[105] in a crimson dawn. I felt truly insignificant crawling my way westward on this fragile quest.

That morning I was feeling low and my motivation was dissipating like the mist. I wondered why my spiritual comfort seemed to ebb away at these liminal moments.[106] Turning back to the path, I felt the cold reach of the mist's icy fingers through my light hiking clothes. Although I had put on virtually every stitch I had, it barely warmed me. I regretted not bringing winter woollies – one of the costs of travelling light. The path continued to rise, gradually working its way up onto a wooded shoulder.

Intense greens, russets and creams – a patchwork quilt of the Asturian farmland – was laid out at my feet. Sparking a memory, my heart ached for home. It was identical to our family farm, which Donal and I had played on as youngsters, and then taken responsibility for when our father died. Once, we had desperately worked to save the harvest after a bad summer. Unfortunately, due to inexperience we had rushed the process and the bales later turned into a musty, fetid mess. I could almost taste failure again now that my own Camino journey was equally disintegrating through injury and lack of fitness. I was enveloped by hopelessness and despair. Disrupted sleep and a minimal breakfast had considerably reduced my energy reserves and I hugged myself against the cold. This day would test the depth of my resolve. It really was 'hard nose the highway'.[107]

The day clouded over and was robbed of any real heat. Despite the early start I was barely able to keep my normal pace. It was a cumulative effect of wear and tear, but also a new weariness now sapped my spirit. I trudged up to an 820-metre crest called Piedratecha (literally 'stone ceiling'), an ominous name given my ever-diminishing abilities. I was overtaken by a Dutch couple who had walked from Irún on the French border as I had. We talked briefly and took a break together on the mountain crest. This was a desolate place, a sandy junction of two trails flanked by stone walls and surrounded by scrub. In contrast to me, the couple seemed in remarkably good shape and eminently confident about an on-time arrival in Santiago. I was beginning to doubt if I would ever escape these endless mountains. From immaculate backpacks they produced flasks of herbal tea and snacks in shiny poly bags. Seeing my meagre salami sandwiches and water, they offered me hot tea, a real treat. On the descent, I lagged behind them as they strode powerfully ahead. I repeated my well-worn mantra, 'Just stick to your own pace.' It was cold comfort, as I could have done with the companionship, especially in this barren place. The eerie swish of windmills on a nearby ridge increased the hostile feeling.

As they stretched out a lead, what looked like a wild mink suddenly ran out directly in front of me and straight down the path towards the oblivious couple. I called out but they scarcely had time to turn around and it was gone. A few seconds of precious wildness – it lifted me. The loping aquiline form of vibrant black fur was a shocking intrusion on a dusty farm track. 'There are some rewards to trailing behind', I thought. The rest of the day was a hard slog though, winding upwards through coniferous forest that gradually became a tunnel of interwoven vegetation. Wary of my legs cramping again, I was doing stretches every hour and walking at an ever-slower pace.

I came to a fork in the road high up on a steep pine-covered hillside, with a sign pointing to a monastery below. The Camino followed the high ground but I deliberately took the downhill sidetrack to see the Obona monastery, which dated from around the thirteenth century. It was listed as 'unmissable' in my guidebook but I grumbled having taken it, as I knew I would have to backtrack uphill to this same point. It was to prove disappointing however, as it was almost totally in ruins, full of ashes and rubble, and badly neglected. The cloister was mostly collapsed, but there was a largely intact nave. I managed to shelter there during a heavy downpour and have something to eat. This Cistercian monastery had been a huge educational, economic and agricultural centre of power in its day, and had been an important refuge for

Camino pilgrims. It was a far cry from that now; rather it had a sense of desolation and desecration.

The feeling of being damp, cold and worn out seemed to symbolise my day; it really was closing in on me from all sides. I felt that I didn't have much left to give and wondered would I be able to finish. Was I just postponing the inevitable by stubbornly refusing to give in? One persistently seductive thought was 'You won't be able to keep doing this for another day, let alone two weeks .... No one would blame you if you were to quit.'[108] After all, even the Cistercian monks had given up on this once holy place.

Having to retrace my steps to pick up the Camino again was dispiriting. The next few kilometres took me through a silent pine forest, a cushion of fragrant needles underfoot. It was temporary relief, being 'held' in a pine tunnel, a rare comfort in a craggy landscape. Eventually, I came to an asphalt road and reluctantly had to put in some 'tarmac time' on it, my muscles complaining. In the middle of this penitential stretch I was greatly cheered when a taxi honked at me and two people waved frantically out the back. It was Frederick and Anton, my two friends from the previous night, who were skipping these next difficult stages as they said they would. Happy for them, it hit me what a relief it would be to be transported; not to have to actually walk, to succumb to the comfort. Mostly, I wanted not to have to spend time alone – what once ironically I craved. Painfully aware of the asceticism involved in my pilgrim existence, I craved mindless diversions and the warm company of friends.

After about thirty minutes of grim slog I came on the tiny village of Campiello, high up on a lofty ridge. The views were dramatic in all directions as a ring of rugged peaks dominated the skyline. Though it was still fairly early, I decided to stop here as it was the only *albergue* for miles, and the guidebook darkly hinted at difficult terrain ahead. I collapsed onto a stool in virtually the only place in town, a garish pink-and-white restaurant called Casa Herminia. Crowded already, like an Irish rural bar it had a raucous but friendly feel. Legs of ham and mutton were hanging by the door, little pools of congealed blood below them. Alongside were agricultural implements, straw hats and tourist postcards; a complete grocery store took up another wall. I had some lovely crusty tuna pie, but having no appetite was unable to finish it.

A young German hiker came in, still glowing from the trail, and, as there were no free seats, I invited him to sit with me. As he spoke excellent English, we got to talking. I noticed him eyeing my leftover pie, and offered him the rest of it, which he readily accepted and soon devoured. He filled me in on the *albergue* here, attached to the restaurant. I gathered that the owner, Doña Herminia, was a materialistic character, charged a bit over the odds (€10) and was not universally liked by hikers. He also told me that the next stage was particularly challenging over rock-strewn trails and had no habitation along the way. It was the infamous 'Roof of the Camino' route to El Palo, a brutal climb,[109] which sounded very menacing. I couldn't shake off a sense of dread that something serious was coming down the line for me. The German decided to go on to the next *albergue* and take the risk that the small hostel there might be already full. I didn't even consider it, bidding him *'Buen Camino'*. I decided to call it a day and stay where I was. 'Play it safe', I thought, as I put off thinking about the next day.

Despite my German friend's caution, Doña Herminia was positively mentioned in my guidebook, which recommended her food and her hospitality. I sought her out, this dynamo who ran the *albergue* and restaurant, and most of the village by the sounds of it. She was lively and engaging but stress was written in her eyes. She took me on a tour of her 'estate', which made up half the village. It consisted of a guesthouse of private rooms and also a conventional pilgrim hostel, which seemed to be a converted barn. She was certainly making the most of the Camino boon that had presented itself. I signed in and got my all-important pilgrim stamp. Having had enough of noisy dorms and poor sleep, I opted for one of the private rooms (€27), which were narrow, sparsely furnished prefabs built into the side of the barn.

Once I settled into my room, I went for a walk around the village, a typical farming outpost with agricultural supplies, barns and a few simple residences on the main street. Vertiginous drops on the northern side defied any farming attempts. This all added to the isolated, lofty feel of the place, a cold, dramatic mountain eyrie. The talk in the *albergue* below me was all about how to negotiate the difficult next stage. I tried not to think about it. Rather, I went back and distracted myself, listening to some music, but nothing satisfied. Normally, the sounds from nature were all the music I needed, but now I desperately wanted diversion.

A heavy mist shrouded the buildings and farms. With the cold and the wind it transformed this country place into something more sinister. 'It might have been a mistake to get a single room and cut myself off so drastically from others', I thought. At 8 p.m. I made my way across the eerily deserted street to Herminia's restaurant. My stomach growling, I had been eating snacks to stave off the gnawing hunger. I could see the clearer outlines of the restaurant now that it was empty. It was actually a homely combination of a bar, a grocery shop and a hardware shop in true Irish style – a one-stop convenience store where you could chat, drink, eat, network and shop all from the one barstool. No doubt this was the locale where everything happened in the area (there was no real competition!). As I waited for my standard *menu del día* there were a few barflies in the corner. Two bartenders were serving, one of whom had Down's syndrome and the same ruddy complexion as Doña Herminia. I was the only outsider. It was a bit unnerving to eat alone. Where were all the other hikers?

The food, when it arrived, was wonderful. Herminia herself served it, and she had probably made it as well. It was *empanadas* (stuffed pastries, typical of the northwest region of Spain), a stew of beans and meat, cured ham and cheese salad, red wine and rice pudding (my favourite) to finish. She hovered round like a mother, saying, 'You have to eat it all up.' It was one of the best hostel meals I got on the Camino. I also got Herminia's undivided attention. She had worked out from my registration that I was a priest and we had a conversation about young people today, the state of the church, married priests, and so on. Eventually, she turned to personal issues in her life. I confess that I had misjudged Herminia, being too ready to believe my German friend's criticisms. I remembered that the word 'prejudice' comes from *pre-judging* someone. Once we got to talk in depth, I could see that there was a lot more to her.

I quickly picked up that she was committed to helping pilgrims and creating a clean, inviting hostel (most had been the exact opposite so far). Amazingly, she did a lot of the day-to-day work herself. She told me about how she served in the shop, cooked the meals, looked after the hostel, and also looked after her elderly mother, who had dementia. As she outlined the contours of her life of service, I could see the weight of anxiety and responsibility written on her face. There was no mention of any man in her life – it was a solo operation by the looks of it. I was greatly humbled by her trust in me, by how much she needed to talk, and by the crushing weight of her daily round. I promised to pray for her in Santiago. I got up to leave with a heavy heart; there was so much silent suffering and stoicism in the world. It brought me right back to my own quest and interior pain; I fled, needing some respite.

The loneliness of my little rustic room settled in around me. There was an ache in my heart from all that this day had brought – the sense of impending doom, a terrifying trail ahead, my own dwindling energy and the hopelessness of my task. The obstacles ahead took on gargantuan proportions as I felt my meagre abilities petering out. I would never be able to keep up the pace needed to punch through the roof of the Camino. For the first time, I seriously considered quitting. Just thinking about it brought me some relief and a sense of escape from the pain. I texted a close friend of mine that I was thinking of stopping to test the idea out on him. 'This is it,' I thought, 'this is where it all comes to an inglorious end.' My Spanish odyssey had reached a real crux, forced to surrender by the imposing Asturian mountains.

The only thing I dreaded now was doing my night prayer (Review of the Day), as my mind had already congealed around the decision to stop. Tired of it all, I wanted it to be nice and simple, and have God go along with my decision. I sat down on the bed reluctantly, fighting the impulse to lie down and immerse myself in sleep. As I went back over the day from Tineo to here, I clearly saw all the dark moments: the cold start, the killer hills, the wasted detour to the monastery, the dull pace, the shroud of mist and the isolation. There had been some 'lights' – the mink appearing, talking to Herminia – but they were few, at least it seemed to me. I knew that the prayer needs to begin with God's view of the day and so I struggled to find some gratitude in myself.[110] I quickly realised that I had been in a low and pessimistic mood all day. I had essentially picked up on all the notes of discouragement and defeat that I came across. With a jolt, I understood that I was experiencing what Ignatius calls 'desolation', a loss of peace and a disturbing unease.[111] This accurately summed up my entire day – a subtle undermining negativity. No wonder I was for packing it in!

Immediately I thought of Donal, who had been similarly overrun by negativity in his life.[112] I had seen at first hand the corrosive effects of the depression that ate away at his soul, imposing a cruel black filter on reality. He had struggled to interpret his increasingly bleak thoughts, sometimes being able to get perspective but mostly sliding into an angry emotional cesspit. I had tried unsuccessfully to be the corrective counterbalance, to point out the kink in the lens, but the negativity was too strong. Still, I felt responsible after his death. I could readily recall all the things I wish I had done differently. The last years I saw him given more and more to the 'dark side', a world of interior agony that those who loved him could only observe with helpless horror. This was desolation writ large, I realised, my brother internalising a deceptively negative perspective of life.

I remembered that Ignatius had a series of guidelines about handling desolation, and the key one was not to change a decision that you had made previously in consolation.[113] This is not to say that details can't be changed (as I had done earlier on the Camino), but these key decisions – the crucial supports for our lives – which were made in peace and positivity, should not be undone in a low moment. I had this image of a tower that I was hanging onto while a gale blew. I didn't want to mess with the tower now that I was feeling the force of the wind. I calmed down and some peace returned. I knew instinctively that I had to hand this whole trip over to God, to something greater than myself, to be able to continue.[114] God was my only support now. As I began to plan for getting back on the road the next day, my mood and spirits rose. 'That was a close call', I thought, 'I almost abandoned the whole thing.' I felt gratitude towards Ignatius for getting me back on track, teaching me to see things through God's eyes. I had been given another chance, one of many on this unpredictable trip. Virtually on cue, my phone beeped and it was a reply from my friend simply saying, 'Don't give up.' Touched, my eyes welled up and I wept. Rolling into bed, I slept well.

Saving Sarah

Everything hurt that morning as I awoke to a grey and drizzly day that reflected my mood. I unenthusiastically scraped the disparate pieces of my gear together and closed the door on yet another hostel. I had a quick breakfast in Herminia's bar, greeting her like an old friend at this stage. I polished off the eggs and bread quickly. It was strange – although I had only arrived the day before, I felt like I had lived a lifetime in this village. I found leaving difficult, always being the one saying goodbye, always going ahead to the next destination.

Still shaken by the watershed that had been Campiello and how close I came to giving up, I tentatively took to the road again. Deep down I knew that my own resources were threadbare and that this Camino, this quest, was in the hands of God now. It was humbling and painful confronting my own limits, and scarily liberating in terms of not knowing what was coming next. I repeated the familiar words 'Into your hands, O Lord, I commend my spirit',[115] spoken by Jesus on the cross at the hour of his death. In a strange way the whole experience on the misty mountain the previous day had been a 'death' for me. Now I was almost surprised to be alive and on the move again, albeit gingerly, but one thing was for sure: I was very grateful for the small wonders of being healthy, mobile and relatively intact.

I knew that I was going to have to take to the hills again, not something I relished. I grimly read in the guidebook that the next section was the most difficult yet. Ominously, it was described as 'a leg breaker', 'not to be done in the rain' and 'not to be done alone'.[116] I mentally ticked off the boxes in my head: I have breakable bones, it is raining and I am alone. Once again, I found myself weighing up the options in Ignatian style. The key for me was to make a good decision, given the reality of my abilities, and not to be seduced by false motivations. In my life generally I was tired of pushing myself too hard and paying the price; the Camino was showing me this clearly.

Ignatius himself, while at Manresa in Spain in 1522–1523, came to understand that his severe and excessive penances were not good (he did some lasting damage) and that he needed to find a more balanced way. Eventually he realised that he was being seduced by the extremes – things that were good in themselves (fasting, penance), but which taken to the extreme were damaging. Ignatius came to understand the importance of 'indifference': being free of one's own agenda in order to listen to what God was saying. This radical freedom to do God's will was what I sought now.[117]

First though, I had to get at all the 'unfreedoms' or resistances within me. To begin with, the unwritten Camino 'rule' that you have to 'walk all the way' had a certain grip on me. Examining it in the light of my predicament, it seemed very unconvincing, as it had already gotten me injured before. In terms of the pilgrimage, it was a 'nice to have', not a requirement.[118] It seemed better to me to assess my present health and fitness and make a decision from there, looking within rather than without. Also, I knew from bitter experience it was better not to push myself to the extreme[119] directly after having had a break or health crisis. It seemed prudent to not put myself in a situation of risk when I was feeling fragile and not fully fit. For all those reasons I didn't take the high road, and instead got a lift to the next town, Pola de Allande. I was to sleep for the rest of the day; it certainly did me no harm.

Pola de Allande is a very curious town. I saw it first from the road high above as it uncoiled its way into a dense nest of buildings in a narrow river valley. With the very high-sided hills around, it gave the impression of having been shoe-horned into the River Nison's steep ravine. The town dates from the thirteenth century and owed much to the migratory cattle trade that dominated its upper hills. It had 'country' written all over it (like most of Asturias) and, though this was heartening, there was something dark and dour about the town that was hard to separate from my listless mood. Constant rain and drizzle didn't help. I dodged from sodden veranda to doorway trying to get a sense of the place, but eventually gave up. After a while ruminating in my room, I just wanted to get away from this place.

A strong memory came to me of the devastation visited on my family and on me in the fallout from Donal's death. There was the numbness and the shock of what happened in the immediate aftermath,[120] but what I didn't foresee was the absolute pit of distress in the years that followed. Long after the rituals and memorial cards were filed away, there was this desperate wound that defied understanding or healing. Suicide affords no luxuries and the lesion remains open, the nerve ends exposed in a brutal lack of healing or closure. The various areas of my life – work, relationships, health and prayer – all took a nosedive. The thread and fabric of life, once so rich in meaning, fell away to reveal the ugliness of existence. Life became an agony of moments and a clawing through the days.

The sudden, violent, unannounced exit of Donal from our lives left us all bereft and beaten, wondering by what personal failures we had contributed to this catastrophe. As the oldest and as a priest I felt acutely responsible – guilt and blame took a hold of me. I, in turn, lashed out at God: 'How could you have let this happen?', 'You promised to protect me, to protect him?', 'Where were you on that darkest of nights that wrecked our lives so completely?' There were no answers, only an awful silence and the drift into depression that goes with hopelessness.

I came back to the current reality as the evening light washed out through the skylight. With a sudden realisation, I knew I was faced with a sharp dilemma. I was now running out of time: I only had ten days left till my flight home and I still had over 220 kilometres to go. With some of the toughest walking directly ahead of me, I had to face some tough decisions (again). I shared my troubles over coffee with a Spanish couple I had met, Marga and Manolo. Once again, they were Camino regulars and I had the feeling they were not impressed with me. (I suspected they were tough trekker regulars who were not into my tardy tactics.) They bluntly put my options to me thus:[121]

- Abandon the Camino now.
- Walk on and see how far you get.
- Skip a few stages ahead and ensure you arrive in Santiago de Compostela in time.

I pondered on these mutually exclusive options. Considering the first one of abandoning the Camino had a dramatic effect on me – I reacted strongly against it; I had come so far through so many different crises that I wasn't for quitting now. The second option was intriguing but starkly put. Effectively this is what I had been doing, ambling along and putting off the impact of all my delays. It was appealing but there was a false ring to it when I realised I would never actually get to Santiago, I would come up some 100 kilometres short. It was only in considering the third option that I felt a fire ignite in my belly.[122] I really wanted to get to Santiago, not because of any trivial need to complete the walk or prove anything, but because I wanted to deliver Donal's T-shirt there. I had promised my brothers and sisters that I would do this and I intended to deliver on my promise. It was more important to me than reputation or glory or fame. I had drifted a little off-course on this quest in falling behind but now I had clarity again, and incredibly I had a window whereby I could still make it in time.

I thanked the Spanish couple and beat a hasty retreat to my room – I needed to make plans. Shaking off a sense of guilt and shame at 'breaking one of the rules', I decided to take public transport the following day to the next city, Lugo. I went down and checked with reception what transport options were available for the morning and then began the familiar packing routine. I now felt charged with a new sense of urgency and optimism; it was like an effervescent current had been introduced into the gloom. I was on a mission again! I would be glad to shake off the traces of this town and its murkiness. However, I had learned some important lessons and gained some valuable insights here; I was grateful.

The next morning saw me out on the footpath with backpack in hand, anxious for the departure. It wasn't going to be easy to get out though as I was still deep in the mountains and there was little transport or infrastructure. The only option was a bus to a nearby town around mid-morning so I had to wait. It was raining as I approached the bus shelter and the sky was a steel grey. Once again I felt the oppression of the place, hemmed in as we were by steep hills all around. There was a young Dutch woman already there, Sarah, obviously a hiker and apparently in trouble with her feet. She had bandaged heels, was wearing open sandals and had trouble walking. It turned out that the heavy mountain boots she began in were shredding her heels and toes. She told me she couldn't put up with the pain anymore and was going where I was going, to Lugo, to buy new boots.

Like many Camino conversations we dispensed with the small talk and got straight to the heart of things. As we got talking she shared with me that she had had a fairly traumatic experience right at the start of the Camino and had been through the mill. This had been an attempted sexual assault at the very beginning of the Camino, virtually on her first day. I felt for her and sensed that she was close to quitting, given so many obstacles in her path. I didn't realise it clearly at the time, but her journey and mine were to become briefly intertwined, getting through these mountains and out to freedom for both of us. Another Spanish woman, who had damaged her knee and had just been to the doctor that morning, joined us at the bus stop. It really was the confraternity of the 'walking wounded', the casualties of the Camino, and I had to count myself among them.

We took the bus to the village of Grandas de Salime, and what a ride it was. There was the initial torturous grinding climb out of the valley to a lofty sky road. When we weren't in a whiteout mist at 1,000 metres, we were racing along vertiginous ridges and taking stomach-churning hairpin bends. Apart from the white-knuckle ride, the journey managed to reveal some of the most beautiful mountain country, with a *Lord of the Rings* quality. Forested ridges, alpine meadows and isolated homesteads stretched off as far as the eye could see. Getting into town was a relief though as I was fairly green at that stage, needing some time to recover over a cola.

Soon, Sarah was urging me on, very keen to get to civilization quickly and to get her feet sorted out. I realised at this stage that we were a team and that my mission, as she didn't speak Spanish, was to be her translator and guide to get her where she needed to go. The problem was that we were in yet another little highland town without onward bus connections. We needed to get across to another mountain town, A Fonsagrada (meaning 'sacred fountain', whose origin is

attributed to St James the Apostle), to make the vital bus connection to Lugo.

Charged up, I went into the first shop that was open on
the main street, an old-style bookshop, where I met the nicest
two women. They told me that the only means of getting to
A Fonsagrada was by taxi and, coincidentally, the husband
of one of the women was a taxi driver. I was getting on so
well with them that Sarah had to come in and get me. Within
a few minutes, the taxi pulled up and we piled in our hiking
gear. I was beginning to enjoy this new adventure and my
new travelling companion; things were working out rather
better than I had hoped.

The journey only took twenty minutes, again at an altitude of 1,000 metres (i.e. the same as the highest mountain
in Ireland), but it was done at high speed and with uncom-
promising cornering. I felt like we were crossing some great
forbidding desert, escaping some terrible badlands, or flee-
ing from some desperate foes. The dramatic geology, the
remoteness and the barren uplands seemed to mirror the difficult experiences we had both been through in the previous
days. I understood the importance of changing the environment as a symbol for inner movement and openness to new
possibilities.

The exhilarating taxi ride delivered us to A Fonsagrada,
where we would get the all-important bus to our destination, Lugo. The only problem was that the departure was
not for four hours; all that speed was for nothing. One
thing the Camino teaches is the art of wasting lots of time
in public places, and so we walked until we found a park
shaded by oak trees and with some benches. We shared our
simple pilgrim fare, some fruit, bread, olives and cheese. The
conversation ranged from our experiences on the Camino,
which was always so diverse, to the inevitable medical ail-
ments that plagued us. It was particularly painful to watch
Sarah hobble around on her lacerated feet, which I hadn't
really noticed until now.

Then the conversation took a deeper turn as Sarah took out a prayer book and told me what she did for a living.[123] It transpired that my new pilgrim friend was actually an Anglican minister and a theologian. Imagine my surprise and then hers as I filled her in on my being a Jesuit priest and school chaplain. There was something apt and ironic about this situation, being travellers from very different backgrounds on the same road and being thrown together in this way. We passed the time very enjoyably, tackling different theological and ecumenical points, but it was on the topic of prayer that we found agreement. Eventually we settled ourselves to read the office from her *Book of Daily Prayer*. I found it surprisingly like the Divine Office I was used to. We passed the book back and forth reading psalms and epistles. At one stage I was amazed to see her produce her Bible as she sought out a Gospel text. The text was one well known to me:

Blessed are they who mourn: for they shall be comforted. Blessed are they that hunger and thirst after justice: for they shall have their fill. Blessed are the merciful: for they shall obtain mercy. Blessed are the clean of heart: for they shall see God.[124]

Read in that context alongside my crippled companion, the words took on an increased meaning and import. I could keenly identify with my twofold mission, both as the grieving brother and now as the humble helper.[125] I saw a tear escape from under Sarah's sunglasses and I knew the words had hit home with her too.

Eventually the long-awaited bus arrived and we took our seats for the third leg of that momentous day. This was to be a testing journey, getting baked by the evening sun on a stiflingly hot minibus, with little or no views. At one stage I was excited to see my friends Frederick and Anton sitting at a roadside bar. I waved frantically at them and gestured wildly to meet them up ahead, but they seemed to be dazzled by the sun and disappointingly didn't react. The countryside became more pedestrian with the descent, and was less stark as we came down out of the high mountains towards Lugo. We had escaped the mountains and whatever paralysis it had exerted on us.

To celebrate our escape we had a pilgrim meal and a glass of wine together in the twilit main square. Then we went our separate ways as I was for walking the next day and she was for buying new boots. Part of the pain of the Camino is the intensity of encounters followed by separation as journeys diverge. That night, doing my Review of the Day (Examen), I felt that God had been very close to me all day. I felt I had made the right decision to jump ahead in the Camino and meeting Sarah was a real bonus. Whatever help I might have given to her, I felt I had received much more. It had awakened something in me that I long feared had been extinguished. Specifically, accompanying Sarah had restored my sense of compassion and care for others, something that suicide grieving had robbed me of.

13

Deliverance

I opened my weary eyes and wondered where I was. The hotel ceiling and the narrow little room swam into focus, and eventually I remembered the previous day's bus journey to Lugo with Sarah. As my body creaked out of bed, I thought 'my last week' with some excitement. I really wanted it finished quickly at this stage and 100 kilometres sounded doable in four fast days. Little did I know what was ahead of me.

As I scraped it together, all my gear looked a bit rough and I looked rough too. I decided not to look in mirrors any more. I got a quick coffee and a croissant in the cafeteria downstairs, my pack at my feet, and was on the road by 7.30 a.m. There was a thick mist and the dull, flat light made the Roman walls and gates even more imposing. The bitter cold had me hurry along to get warm. Initially, I had trouble finding the Camino markers – the scallop shells – set into the pavement. Eventually I caught up with two tall Spanish hikers. They had this amazing slow, relaxed lope that was deceivingly efficient, as I was to find out. They directed me ahead through the city walls, but in my haste I forgot their directions and ended up following a circuitous route that brought me out behind them once more. 'More haste, less speed', I thought.

Somehow, I had lost my own relaxed rhythm and was back in race mode, some of it brought on by 'finishing fever'. Also however, a certain amount of exhaustion was clouding my judgement. On the way out of town I passed a group of three Spanish women who would shortly overtake me as I stopped to do my stretches by the broad River Miño. There was a worrying jagged pain developing in my left calf muscle and no amount of stretching seemed to ease it. I bitterly regretted going too fast earlier, but I just had to let go of this now. Ignatius would have counselled me to be free and detach from this corrosive emotion in order to deal well with the present. I looked up to my right where a 20-metre-wide floating bridge had been constructed right across the river. Curiously, it was fitted with ladders, seats and decking, effectively turning the whole river into a swimming pool. It looked a bit crazy to me; normally I would have inspected it closely but I was more interested in getting walking again.

I had just wanted an easy saunter towards Santiago, but now I faced a battle to see how far my leg would take me. I had hoped for a wooded track but instead was subjected to a tarmac surface and a quiet back road. I had also hoped for a little café along the way but there was none. All these hopes were killing me now, as I struggled to let go. Thankfully I fell into step with one of the Spanish women I had passed earlier. I was grateful for the company and how the distance shortened with the chat. She and her two friends had just started that day (Monday) and were looking to get to Santiago by Wednesday! I admired such optimism and certainty. One of them, setting herself up as the leader, was striding ahead at a brutal pace. I reflected on how often I had done this, trying to force reluctant pilgrims up mountains in Ireland. I could see the folly of it now and the lack of tolerance and compassion it espoused. I resolved to do things differently when I got back.

Eventually I had to let them go, slowed by pain as I was, and gradually was overtaken by all the others.

With no pilgrims and no traffic, the little Galician country road suddenly became terribly lonesome. I could feel that familiar dreaded muscular spasm in my calf that I knew only too well, a crippling stabbing pain that rippled out as the muscle contracted. I tried to ignore it for a while and keep up a moderate but hobbling pace. It only worsened so I stopped to do some more stretching, rubbed on some anti-inflammatory cream and did some massage on it. Nothing worked. A certain tide of panic rose within me as well as deep frustration and resentment – it was so unfair. I gasped for air, struggling to let these feelings subside.

Unable to walk, I cast off my rucksack. 'This is it', I thought, 'This is where it all ends. The Camino is over for me; now I'll have to go home.' The bitter thought was laced with some relief and resignation, as I conceded, 'I just want the pain to stop.' Another part of me was outraged and frustrated with the constant injuries and enforced stops that got in the way of progress. I had to really force myself to go into a deeper place away from the morass of anger, blame, escapism and avoidance. Thinking of Ignatius sick and wounded gave me some distance to get perspective on what I doing. I formed a little prayer: 'Over to you Lord, I am totally out of options here.'

Feeling a bit more centred, I thought to myself, 'Hold on, before giving up totally, let's look at the options here. What can I actually do?' I gazed around for inspiration. I thought I might get a lift but there was no traffic, only trees all around and no civilization. Alone and isolated, eventually I realised that I was going to have to get myself out of this. What to do? I reckoned that I could, ignoring the pain, probably hobble on for another 2 to 3 kilometres maximum. It was too far to go back to Lugo. It was a bit frightening, knowing that I had to find help soon; if not I was in real trouble. Still, I felt God hadn't let me down so far. I got up, gritting my teeth, and using my pole as a crutch began a lame shuffle at a snail's pace. Then the rain came on and I kept focused as best I could, trying to dispel the despairing thoughts. It was the longest walk on a hard road.

A memory came to me of Donal, when he had had a breakdown. I was at home helping him on the farm and I had also arranged some medical appointments for him, one of which was with a specialist in Derry, some two hours away. We set off in our old diesel car and, running late as usual, I overtook a number of cars on a rare straight stretch (with Donal egging me on, I might add). Then, to my horror, an oncoming SUV appeared, heading straight for me, and I couldn't get back into the line of cars. Only for the SUV driver swerving off the road and driving onto the verge, it would have been a head-on collision. I pulled in on the same verge and came to a stop in some shock, my fingers buried in the steering wheel like a cartoon character. Donal got out to deflect the wrath of the SUV driver now irately bearing down on us. Here was he batting for me and I was supposed to be looking after him. Strangely, I felt the same now, that my brother was somehow protecting me, that disaster had been averted, and that good could come out of this situation. It gave me strength.

Just when I thought I would pass out or fall to the ground, I came to the tiniest of villages. It was called Burgo and comprised about four farmhouses clustered around a crossroads. I knew I couldn't expect a doctor or pharmacy way out here, but to my enormous relief there was a sign for a bar just down a side road. Grimacing, I limped in the long gravel drive and gasped out my order, '*Café con leche, por favor.*' When I finally shook my attention from my own pain, I was initially repelled by the state of the place in which I found myself. There were legs of smoked ham hanging above a bar counter stained with beer and timbers browned with years of smoke. Flies were buzzing around me in a disconcerting way and the old lady who limped in to attend the bar had an intimidating demeanour in the half-light. I almost panicked. I was stranded here, off the Camino, in an empty bar in a very vulnerable position, unable to walk. I was wary, unsure as to whether I could trust her, yet forced by circumstances to be there.

Just for a moment I had a flash back to the US backwoods movie *Deliverance*, where local inbred Georgia natives attack a group of weekend warrior paddlers. What starts out as a fun outdoor adventure dramatically turns into a nightmare struggle for survival. I thought maybe I had stumbled on some unredeemed corner of Galician wilderness. For a moment, I saw myself skewered, smoked and salted in the rafters. I shrugged the image off, forcing myself to focus on the present. I put the words together for a brief conversation, seeing the bar lady as more benign and human now. I realised the negative effects of the inhuman, agonising walk I had just been on. I remembered one of Ignatius' rules for deciding well: 'Don't make hasty decisions when you're low, but also be proactive against the negativity'[126] so I put my imaginings to one side and gratefully tucked into my milky coffee and biscuits. As my blood sugar levels came up I started to feel substantially better.

Feeling my humanity returning, I struck up a conversation with the bar woman, whose name was Consuelo.[127] She turned out to be very pleasant. However, I quickly got down to the key questions. Did they have any rooms? She said they had a bunk in a lean-to on the roof of the pub. Did they do food? She said she could give me lunch and dinner for a reasonable price. I couldn't believe my luck; 'Thank you, God', I whispered to myself. Warming to the newly emerging situation, I asked the key question: did she have some painkillers? She kindly offered me her own prescription medicine for her bad hip; she was generosity herself! I quickly downed one of the sachets mixed with water, seeking some relief from my throbbing persistent leg ache. Before long however, I realised that her medicine was about six times stronger than normal. However, I wasn't feeling any pain, and that was the first time that day. I marvelled at how the day had turned around from the edge of disaster, how I had everything I needed in this rustic pub, and how my own emotions and preconceptions had been the biggest barriers. It was a radical lesson in trusting in providence, in goodness, even in the most unlikely setting. It was 10 a.m., the most eventful part of the day was over and all was well with the world.

I took my second coffee outside to some chunky garden seats that I guessed had been made in the wood shop next door (dismissing any 'chainsaw massacre' images). A soulful-eyed mongrel lay at my feet, the sun warmed my back and all was bliss. The silence was broken by the arrival of a group of four Belgian undergrad students who were looking for beer. Once they placed their order we introduced ourselves and inevitably the talk turned to the Camino. They were on their first day and wanted to walk the last 100 kilometres as the minimum to get the official certificate, the *Compostela*. With the optimism of youth they were determined to reach Santiago in three days, pretty ambitious. When I questioned this, one responded flatly, 'We have to get there.' As I looked at their flip-flops, their big rucksacks, and the cans of beer strapped on top, I certainly wished them all the best and prayed for them.

Consuelo, meantime, couldn't have been more pleasant and helpful, dispelling completely my initial misconception. She brought me upstairs to my bunk, which was in a bizarre annex actually on the roof of the pub. It was a familiar hostel-type room with two bunks but I would have the room to myself. I could hardly believe my luck. After a delightfully long and pain-free siesta I came down for the trusty *menu del día*, the three-course lunch prepared by Consuelo. Famished after the day I had had, I was ravenously hungry. She brought out a mixed tuna salad with lots of olives to start; the main course was a tender cut of veal with chips and greens; and the dessert was a simple bowl of ice cream, but this was a step up from the normal tub of yogurt. Desserts had been a bit poor on the Camino but at €10 for everything, including a glass of wine, I wasn't complaining. One of the great pleasures of the Camino is being grateful for your food, the fruit of hard walking, and a heightened awareness of the wonderful activity of eating.

A large man dressed in heavy work clothes was eating at another table and by following the conversation I deduced that he was Consuelo's husband, Jaime. He ran the huge carpentry workshop right next to the pub. Again, if I was to go on his appearances (scruffy, dour, withdrawn) he was an axe-murderer, but fortunately I had already learned that lesson. We got on great and he took me for a tour of the workshop. Then, the two of us became engrossed in a dubbed Sean Connery film, *Outland*, which was showing on the television in the corner. It was a surreal space-western, but it provided some much-needed escapism. After the film, Jaime took himself outside and lay down on a bench, where he was soon fast asleep.

Feeling considerably better, I asked Consuelo what there was to see around here; the village itself was a huddle of houses barely 100 metres long. She directed me to an old church in the woods nearby. It took me a long time to find it; the country lane leading there was the epitome of tranquillity and I was lost in gratitude for the wonder of creation, me being alive and being able to walk gingerly.

I had walked past it before I realised it; unsigned and practically invisible, it was set back from the road. It was beautiful in its simplicity, probably built in the seventeenth or eighteenth century, almost completely constructed of stone with a few timbers. There was such an atmosphere of peace and calm in the glen that I speculated that the chapel was once on the Camino. It certainly lulled me into reflection and I came back to myself, feeling rooted and centred after a chaotic morning. I made my way back to the pub again and I still had five hours of daylight. I began to read *The Count of Monte Cristo* on my phone in a little chair on the pub rooftop. It was a long but serene evening.

That night I did my Examen of the day as usual in my bunk. Even though it had been a day of crisis and near disaster, it had all turned around on that simple decision to keep going on the road. I was filled with gratitude not only for the gift of being able to break an old habit of being panicked into poor decisions, but for the wisdom of St Ignatius' method of reflection. I felt that something really important had happened and I was filled with a warm gratitude that permeated my disposition and attitudes towards that day. It was like I was discovering his Examen prayer anew. Like the famous Jesuit leader, Pedro Arrupe, I understood the words: 'More than ever I find myself in the hands of God.'[128] I knew now that the Camino was out of my hands; it wasn't my project any more. I was handing it over, and was very comfortable with that.

The next morning I woke up around 7 a.m. to the splash of running, cascading water. I was confused initially, trying to remember where I was (On top of the pub in a flimsy annex, unveiled itself in my mind). I thought it was someone having a shower nearby but when I got up to peer out the window, I realised it was a real deluge of rain hopping off the tarred roof. There being nothing I could do, I sank back into the soft duvet and went back to sleep. When I eventually got up at 8.30 and went down to the bar for breakfast, it was full of drenched pilgrims. Having hardly seen a soul there the day before, it was strange to see so many together forced in by the rain. I was the only one in dry gear, everyone else was soaked. Amazingly, my leg felt good again – all that rest, painkillers and diversion seemed to do the trick.

Having had a *café con leche* and some amazing chocolate croissants (one of the Camino's little pleasures), I bid Consuelo a warm and grateful goodbye. I had learned a lot in this unlikely place about trust and how to let go of judgements; it had been a real deliverance for me. Back on the Camino, I set off, slowly this time, thinking maybe I would manage a realistic 10 kilometres that day.

As I looked back on this little insignificant hamlet, I realised that I had learned more and been transformed more here than anywhere else. The defining moment was my calf injury and being stranded on the road; I was literally forced to let go and to let God operate. Great things certainly came out of it, exactly what I needed in fact. Then there was the overcoming of my fears and stereotypical judgements about Consuelo and her husband. And yet they couldn't have been more caring, generous and accommodating – they provided for all my needs. I noticed my initial negative reaction to them as different, a writing them off without knowing them, which came out of fear and prejudice. Instead, I had so much to be thankful for. St Ignatius used to say that the lack of gratitude was the only real sin.[129] I knew the truth of this out on the Galician Camino. I consciously remembered what this humble family had done to get me miraculously back on the road. I resolved to be a more grateful person, to acknowledge all that I have received and to live in the glow of gratitude as Ignatius recommends in the Examen prayer.

Carried by Kindness

I was getting pretty tired of it all at this stage so it was really hard to drag myself out of my hostel bunk in the morning. It hadn't helped that I had felt cold during the night – the hostel only had one blanket for me and I rued leaving my sleeping bag behind to keep the weight down. Then the early risers had departed as subtly as a herd of elephants with hobnail boots. As I was organising my by now distinctly grubby gear, a guy leaned down from a nearby bunk and asked me what sounded like 'How's your food?'

'My food', I thought, looking at my plastic bag of groceries; 'Have we mice too?' Then I realised that he, a Portuguese man, was asking me about my *foot* and that I had met him ten days ago on the Camino. He and his girlfriend, the most Irish looking redhead, invited me to have breakfast with them. I was mighty glad as I was low on food and I sorely needed some companionship to help me get going. Sharing breakfast was never so much about human warmth and so little about food, although the calories helped too. I gave thanks for their humble hospitality.

Reluctantly, I took my leave and headed up the mist-covered mountain to a pass among wind turbines. There was something distinctly *Lord of the Rings* about the tenebrous granite path and the epic quest that I was on.[130] It was bitterly cold in the beginning but I soon warmed up with the exercise and the clearing of the mist. The high pass opened out into a wooded valley and I descended into a green and brown patchwork of rushy fields, pines and moorland. I was grateful that there were no more ascents – I was more than done in and just stumbling along on autopilot.

There was something about this Galician area that was not typically Spanish though. Suddenly it hit me – it was exactly like a bog road near home in Northern Ireland. This really moved me; to feel that I was going home, that I had these familiar landmarks and that I was close to those I loved. I thought of my family and the farm, especially Donal, who was *the* farmer. These were the same roads and fields that we had walked as children out chasing cattle. We were shaped by the landscape, formed from that peaty soil, and sculpted by the elements. Here it was recreated in western Spain to bolster me at this difficult moment.

As usual, I was walking alone for several hours. I then caught up with a family I had seen in the hostel the night before. I noticed that two of the teenagers were limping and they had old nylon frameless packs, which were pulling heavily on their backs. I got talking with the aunt, Mariana, and she explained that they were the Alvarez family, from Mexico, on a European trip. They were four cousins, all teenagers, and she was the only adult. I was impressed by them right off; they were so open and happy in that uniquely Latino way. Chatting away, I got to know them as we walked along, and the kilometres flew. The pain in my feet increased and I stopped for a break, thinking I would return to my own company again. They made to go on, but then the aunt asked me to give them a blessing, knowing I was a priest. They all lined up, heads bowed on this dusty broken path on the Spanish Camino. I was humbled and very moved such that I was barely able to utter an improvised Spanish blessing. 'This is one of those Camino moments for sure', I thought.[131]

I walked on my own for a bit and then in a bar came upon another Portuguese group who had also been in the hostel. They were in high spirits, anticipating finishing soon, and having a few beers (even though it was only 10.30 a.m.); I joined in with the fun and felt the better for it, leaving them to it an hour later. I walked on again, now in increasing heat and back on the asphalt. I caught up with the Alvarez family again, who were going very slowly (they said I was going fast!). I tried to help them adjust their backpacks, which were weighing heavily on their shoulders. We walked the last few kilometres into Melide together, our destination for the day. It was actually the meeting point of our Camino, the *Primitivo*, and the main artery, the *Camino Francés*. Part of me was sad to be leaving the mountains and the solitude, for now we would be walking with hundreds on the final run-in to Santiago, just over 50 kilometres away. It was so close I could hardly breathe – a combination of excitement, emotion and exhaustion.

Afterwards I went to the parish Mass where the priest kindly let me concelebrate. I was delighted to see the Alvarez family there and I blessed them again at the end of Mass, during the pilgrims' blessing. We had a great reunion in the square after Mass, as if we had all known each other our whole lives. The town was full of hikers from all over and every second one was either limping, had a support bandage on or smelled of menthol muscle rub. Many people had blue kinesiology tape on their leg muscles, which gave a new respectability to pulls and strain. There was a sense of greater accumulation of injuries as we neared our sacred destination, and the extent of the sacrifices involved was visibly evident. That evening I bumped into a Belgian guy, Mikael, whom I had met two weeks earlier when he was setting out from Oviedo with his dad. Suffering from severe tendonitis, he had been told by a doctor to stop walking. So here he was waiting for his father to arrive, trying to fill in the time, abstractly watching cycling on television. He was tuned out and disheartened. It was hard to watch, even harder to try to console him.

The next morning, I was on the *Camino Francés* at 7 a.m. and was a bit put out that there were so many people walking already. In fact, from here on I would be saying goodbye to the solitude that I had experienced on the other routes. The morning was overcast and mercifully cool, perfect for walking. I saw all types of people and gear, yet disconcertingly no one I recognised. However, about 10 a.m. I came upon the Alvarez family again, having a snack in the woods. 'This is happening a lot', I thought, but I was happy to join them and share their yogurt and biscuits. I walked with them for a while, now feeling like part of the family. Then I had the mad idea that I would race the youngest boy, Juan Pablo, up the steep incline (they were ribbing me as to who was the fastest walker). He went straight into the lead and I was trying to catch him; I started to run and so did he; and of course he beat me to the top though I pretended I had won. It was great fun – a bit mad in the context, as it took all my residual energy – but it brought us all together.

I reflected that there was something touchingly pure and innocent about this Mexican family. They reminded me of my time in Colombia as a Jesuit student: the real down-to-earth goodness of the Latin Americans, so compassionate, warm and transparent. There was something else too though: they reminded me of Donal before depression and mental illness got their talons into him – he had been such a bright light: smart, entertaining, warm and funny; compassionate and prayerful. Then, inevitably, they reminded me of myself before suicide wreaked its devastation: how I had been similarly open and optimistic, trusting and believing. Was it just naïvety about the world? Could I believe in hope again, was there some rescue after trauma, would negativity be overcome? It hurt to think of these things.

Back on the dusty Camino de Santiago, I just watched these Mexicans and marvelled. They were great fun to be with and they strongly encouraged me to walk with them as we neared our goal. I was torn, especially as I felt very protective of them, but also impatient to get finished. Saying an emotional good-bye, I walked on. After all, I had set out on this walk solo and I didn't want to be picking up passengers so close to the finish. I reminded myself that this was for the best and pushed on, free now, and walking fast again. A little voice questioned whether I was doing the right thing, but I ignored it.[132]

An hour later, I had a leisurely but lonely lunch in Arzúa, the main town. I was pushing hard now, the end almost in sight, and I abandoned my slow pace just to get finished, to get the pain over with. I was in between hostels, and knew that I would have to do a mammoth 15 to 20 kilometres to make the one that would put me in position for finishing in Santiago the next day. I had to pinch myself: Santiago? Finishing? After all this time, suffering and amazing grace, for it to be over. I headed out the road in the noonday sun, trusting that something would come up along the way. After about 6 kilometres I was beginning to wilt and I stopped at a roadside café for an ice cream. I got the impression that it was newly built and specifically for walkers, part of the commercial boon that was the Camino. It was here that I met the indomitable Portuguese group again, and I was might-ily glad of their company. 'Another 5 kilometres' said the woman in the café, and it seemed like an eternity. Around an hour later I came across a sign for a private hostel that was not on the map; it was a godsend.

I thought to myself, 'Am I in paradise?' as I walked through the gates of Pousada de Salceda, an independent hostel on the Camino. There was a fountain in the centre, a state-of-the-art cafeteria and pilgrims sunbathing in the gardens. I was wasted, footsore and weary, seeking refuge. I treated myself to a room that, though basic, seemed the last word in comfort to me. Doing my laundry in the sink was a delight for once as the fountain tinkled outside. I had a celebratory beer at the bar, the breeze taking the edge off the Galician sun, and a lovely dinner alone at a table in the restaurant. That evening, as the sun was setting, I took myself up a nearby hill where I could witness the magnificence of this sundown. The brown, gold and orange tones emanated from the sun, which was setting in the west, virtually directly over Santiago, only 28 kilometres away. I wanted very badly to end this odyssey or survival story, or whatever it had become. But a part of me also dreaded finishing; I didn't want to leave this simple life behind where I felt so close to God and where things made sense, even amid the vulnerable unpredictability. I stayed until there was only a silver rim on the horizon, a visual echo of what once was.

I was moved to think of the last time I had seen Donal alive. It was at the beginning of the summer and he seemed in uncommonly good form. He had moved back into our family farmhouse, living there alone, among the ghosts. Not accustomed to his upbeat mood I put it down to some kind of recovery (in fact, later I learned that this is one of the danger signs; the person has made a plan and intends to execute it, alleviating their normal distress and anxiety).[133] We spent some time together as usual and it wasn't long before I realised that this was not the brother I knew. Fundamentally, there was no connection or nothing of the close relationship that we had had. We would normally tell each other everything, especially about what was going on inside, how we felt. I was disconcerted to think that my brother was slipping away from me, becoming unreachable, but the outer bonhomie seemed to give the lie to that and I chose to believe the latter – that he was recovering. Later, this was a source of great pain, guilt and remorse to me: why did I not recognise the signs, why did I go away on holidays, why didn't I stay around? The bitter aftertaste lingered.

It all started off so well that morning; I was up early and the hostel put on breakfast at 7 a.m. (a rarity in itself).

The azure sky lifted my spirit. I knew I could make it to Santiago in one day if I really pushed it. What could possibly go wrong? Packing my gear after breakfast I began to experience a strange unease and feeling out of sorts. It was a peculiar feeling, especially when contrasted with the inner anticipation of finishing the Camino. I had to sit back and consciously examine what was happening within me. I had to fight against my head saying 'Just ignore all that and push on; quick, quick, you're losing time.' It was a familiar battle to me at this stage, forcing myself to slow down enough to be able to listen to what was really going on inside, the emotional conversation. Ignatius would have been familiar with this when he was convalescing, and was forced by circumstances to listen to the inner voices and discern which was genuinely life-giving and from God.

I knew two things: one was the enormous pressure and excitement of finishing this thing after four weeks on the road and many adventures. I just wanted it to be over and to finally rest, to take off the rucksack and not have to think anymore. The other was this strange empty feeling, that I was missing something, and that I needed to pay attention to it. To be honest, I didn't really want to hear this latter voice at this stage; it wasn't where I was at. However, there was something insistent and wholesomely true about it, something that I had learned not to ignore.

After some time sitting on my bed and wrestling with it, watching the other hikers leaving, it finally came to me: 'It's the Mexican family. They have been inviting you multiple times to join them and you have refused them – now this is literally your last chance to take up that offer.' I didn't quite understand why God was asking me to take up this paradoxical offer, as they seemed fine on their own. I just knew that this was something I had to do. Ignatius would have called my jarring unease 'desolation',[134] the experience of being out of tune with the Spirit and being pestered by God to get with the programme. I delayed my departure by some hours, to let them catch up, and set out on the road to find them.

I ambled along the tree-lined path, not pushing it, having learned some hard lessons in that department. I began to get back into the rhythm, like putting on an old familiar coat. My legs were really feeling it all now and frequently I felt the twinge of some muscle or tendon, so I had to stop to massage the area or do stretches. There was something different this morning though: first, I felt completely out of energy, like there was nothing left in the tank; and second, there was a new sharp pain in the tendon at the side of my left knee. Rather than complain about it, I readily fell into the 'injury' routine – seeking some medical help and finding a place to rest. I slowly wound my way up the hill into a small town called O Pedrouzo. I had only done 6 kilometres and I was finished. Philosophically I thought, 'At this rate I'll be crawling on my hands and knees into Santiago.'

Getting this close to Santiago, I was now seeing the worst of commercialisation. For example, people would appear in the middle of nowhere handing out leaflets for their particular hostel or *pension*. At one point I was crossing a road and a recorded voice bid me welcome on behalf of some hostel in Santiago – I nearly jumped out of my skin. Now in the towns and villages on the *Camino Francés* there was a huge variety of public and private accommodation. Everything was developed around the needs of the passing pilgrim, a far cry from the low-key approach that I had experienced earlier in the Basque Country.

As I passed the municipal hostel in town I was thrilled to see two members of the Mexican family; I had almost given up hope of meeting them again. They were first in a queue for the hostel because they had gotten a lift there that morning as they both had hurt their legs and couldn't walk. They were waiting for their aunt and the other two teenagers. I decided I would keep them company till the others arrived, as they did not know how long they would be. It was the longest afternoon, hot and dusty, but we made the best of it. We played some games, speculated on where the others were and talked about many topics. At one stage I went off to the chemist, where I got a knee support bandage with the now very familiar advice: rest, ice, massage and anti-inflammatories. Rejoining the teenagers back at the hostel, we were joking that the support bandages were infectious as all three of us were now wearing them. It was getting late in the afternoon and I realised they hadn't eaten so I made them some sandwiches from my hiking supply. This simple meal of breaking bread and sharing water moved me to reflect on the Mass; how the life-giving flesh and blood of Christ was a supreme act of love for us. It was the giving of his very self, the ultimate selflessness, that I had witnessed many times on the Camino.

We had an interesting conversation about vocation as they were asking how I came to be a priest; they were all Catholics and intensely interested – not something I was used to at home. At this stage they were getting worried about the others, as they were long overdue. We went through various scenarios and tried to work out what could we do to contact them. Just as we were despairing of the situation, the three walkers arrived in great form and there was a happy reunion. Put off by the huge, impersonal hostel, they decided to stay in a *pension*, and I got a room above theirs. That evening, we all went to Mass together at the local church, firm friends at this stage. The only problem I had was beginning Mass with the other celebrants; they genuflected at the altar, but I only made it halfway down with the agonising pain in my knee. I was really struck with the lovely blessing for pilgrims they had at the end of Mass, and I got to bless the Alvarez family again.

I woke at 6 a.m. and threw open the windows of my room. 'This is going to be it (it has to be)', I thought and, moved to tears, I watched the sun struggling to rise behind a wall of clouds. This would be the end of my struggle, finishing the

Camino. I prayed for a while, just simply handing it all over to God, the suicide and the pain, and I asked for help with the day to come.[135] I had arranged to meet the Alvarez family at 7 a.m. so we could walk together. One of the injured girls, Milli, was getting the bus and would meet us later while one of the boys, José Carlos, had made a miraculous recovery. We set off at a nice pace and were surprised that there were so few on the road. Having had no breakfast, after an hour I had to stop for coffee, just to eat something to get energy. They were good enough to wait for me even though I told them to go on. Round about then I realised that they were carrying me; I was completely done in.

There then began one of the most painful days of walking of my life. It was one thing that I had no energy left and felt totally drained, but another was just the physical pain involved in walking. I don't know whether it was the build-up of lactic acid, accumulated injuries or the prolonged effects of dehydration, but this day sapped all of my meagre resources and will. I felt sick most of the time and the physical pain in my feet was extreme. I felt that I was stumbling along on two stumps for feet and although there was a certain numbness in repeatedly hitting the ground, the pain was always there nonetheless. I had a bitter, acidic taste in my mouth that nothing could wash away, a bitter cup.[136] It was all I could do to keep one foot in front of the other. Again, I was so glad of the company for I was reduced to survival mode and only kept going with the help of my ever-buoyant friends.

A little further down the path, Juan Pablo, the youngest, was complaining about the pain in his feet. He lay down on the road on his back while his cousin, Monica, massaged his feet. I wanted to lie on the road too but I knew I would never get up again. We were all vying to carry his pack to give him a chance to recover, but he doggedly refused. His aunt talked to him on her own, and after some food and a little TLC he made an amazing recovery. We were a fragile enough group of travellers between injuries and exhaustion. Even the weather was oppressive and there were several cloud bursts; we gave up putting on and taking off our rain gear, and just walked in the rain, not really caring.

On this never-ending grey day we walked through increasingly frequent villages and developments for hikers: cafés, hostels and boarding houses. It became very busy on the road with throngs of pilgrims over-running us. There were also many 'bicycle pilgrims', decked out with panniers, flying past us. I was outraged to hear that a bike which was going too fast, unable to stop, had already hit Juan Pablo several days before. It all seemed too busy, fast and frantic. The Camino was now all asphalt with no respite for sore knees and tired tendons.

At this stage the inexhaustible aunt, Mariana, had already fed us a number of times from her bottomless bag, but I was also raiding the automatic vending machines on the roadside for more energy food. We were to meet Milli at a place called Monte de Gozo (Hill of Joy), so called because it is a high point where medieval pilgrims would get their first view of Santiago. It was a disappointing place, however, especially as we couldn't see the city for the cloud and the eucalyptus trees. I wasn't feeling much of that pilgrim joy. The tiny chapel of San Marcos was the only saving grace; we prayed here and got our pilgrim stamps.

We walked to the rusty monument to Pope John Paul II where we met an exuberant Milli. This put us in good spirits and we set out to walk the last 4 kilometres, an hour's walk into Santiago. I would love to say that they were joyous and pain-free but they were not (as befitting the Camino experience). They were gruelling, slow and painful; it was an excruciating dragging of oneself into the city. It was now around 1 p.m.; amazingly we were in the suburbs of Santiago, and incredibly I was starving again. I told Mariana I had to eat and again they were gracious enough to accompany me, right on the cusp of finishing. We had the special pilgrim's menu, not a spectacular meal but all the better for sharing it.

Off we set again for the last 2 kilometres to the cathedral, the focal point. The streets wound uphill in a circular fashion to the old medieval centre. We threaded our way through traffic lights and zebra crossings, now in silence, until we suddenly hit the old part of town. Then it was all downhill on the granite streets, through an archway and suddenly we were out into the square in front of the cathedral with its impressive facade. There was no great celebration or punching the air. They were relieved and I was battered and bewildered, like a sea survivor who is not used to being on dry land.

However, entering the cathedral was an awesome moment. The baroque façade and the Romanesque Pórtico da Gloria (Gate of Glory) are architectural wonders in themselves, but it was seeing the luminous *baldachin* ('cloth of gold') over the altar from the back of the nave that brought me to my knees. I felt like a medieval knight who had completed his quest and was now awed in the presence of his Lord. I was sure the former soldier St Ignatius understood this image when he made his allegiance to Christ, his new Lord. Most of all, I could see the illuminated altar which was where I would place Donal's T-shirt, fulfilling the promise I had made to my siblings and finishing my month-long quest. However, it was too much for me at this time. I got up off my knees to look for my companions.

Together, we made a beeline for the tomb of the Apostle St James (after whom the city is named: *Sant Iago*), underneath the main altar. We prayed a while there and then queued up to ascend the steps to embrace a statue of the apostle that is right behind the altar. We also spent some time in the hushed reverence of the Blessed Sacrament chapel; I was very impressed with the faith of my Latino friends, much stronger than mine. Having missed the Pilgrim Mass for that day, we went to the Pilgrim Office to get our *Compostelas*, the official certificate of finishing the pilgrimage. I found the ritual moving, getting official recognition for being a pilgrim and for finishing, someone recognising the journey I had been on.

The Alvarez family then went off to their *pension*, agreeing that we would meet the next day at the 12 noon Pilgrim Mass. I wanted to take some time to savour this moment and so I went back to the square, found a café that looked onto the cathedral, and had a cold beer. I appreciated everything – the day, the place, the people, my life, the gift of being here now. It was great to sit there and just to be, to watch all the comings and goings, and marvel at it all. It was incredible that I had made it at all and I was deeply grateful to God and all the myriad people who had helped me. I smiled to think of St Ignatius looking down on me and I thanked him for the gift of reflection that had seen me through some tight spots. However, I knew that I had a lot of processing yet to do on this astoundingly complex and layered experience.

I eventually found the Jesuit Community and was dismayed to find that because of an unfortunate mix-up in communications they were not expecting me. The great welcome that I was expecting for the conquering pilgrim hero was cooler than I expected and so it was that I had a very low-key solitary evening unpacking. Everything was strewn around me, creased, filthy and unwashed, pretty much the way I felt. I retired early for a much-needed sleep and collapsed unconscious into a dreamless world.

15

Atonement

My eyes opened from way, way down in a pit where I felt I had fallen in the bed. There was a blanket of tiredness that pressed me down and kept me immobile. Something in the back of my head triggered a sort of psychic alarm that rung persistently – what was it about? Oh yes, it was about the Pilgrim Mass at 12 noon, which I really needed to be at. I struggled with the forces of gravity and sleep deprivation, forcing out my legs and arms from under the cover in what was a huge act of will. Eventually I just sat there on the bed, unhappily bemoaning my fate of being so exhausted yet forced to get up on my first official day off in five weeks.

I remembered the days in the aftermath of Donal's death. I had prayed St Patrick's Breastplate, a prayer of protection that I repeated now:

I arise today through the strength of heaven …[137]

I thought about all the black mornings that those few words got me through, invoking the divine when I was incapable of action myself. I remembered Donal's depression and how he had not been able to 'arise'. However, I was now in Santiago de Compostela, named after the 'field of stars'[138] and theatre of divine promise. This was going to be a good day, a day of 'rising'. After showering, the first thing I put on was Donal's old T-shirt, looking a sorry sight after all that time in the rucksack. I had been forced to wear it once, when I ran out of clothes on the walk, but I felt Donal would understand. I took a moment on the steps of the Jesuit house, holding back the tears. I felt already that this was going to be the moment I had been waiting for, the big release of the burden I had carried all the way from France. It was atonement, an offering of this symbol – the shirt – to erase all the shame and guilt. I knew I was offering myself to be transformed.[139]

Late, I raced down to the cathedral, which was only some minutes away, hoping to be on the altar to concelebrate with all the other priests for the special noon Pilgrim Mass. Even at twenty to the hour it was almost full with a variety of nations, voices and costumes; a Latin American folk group sat in the front row with elaborate headdresses. I frantically searched for the sacristy, having to go all the way around the high altar, thronged with tourists and camera lenses. Eventually I found it at the opposite end; I saw a medieval-dressed steward try to silence the boisterous crowd but to no avail. Inside, there were around sixteen priests from all over the world who were already vesting, to likewise concelebrate the Mass. My heart was beating fast as I slipped on my white alb, concealing Donal's T-shirt from everyone but me. The dean of the cathedral, Padre José Maria Diaz, was handing out assignments and coordinating the huge multicultural celebration. As the only native English speaker I was asked to do one of the Prayers of the Faithful, and to read a small part of the Eucharistic Prayer.[140] In connection with the latter, he handed me a one-page leaflet which had the prayer printed out in English and my section highlighted in yellow:

Lord, remember your Church throughout the world;
Make us grow in love, together with Benedict our Pope,
Julián our bishop, and all the clergy.

But then as I looked below this prayer on the sheet, my heart nearly stopped. I felt the words come up off the page towards me in a rush of emotion. What was written on this A4 dog-eared copy described exactly what I had come here for:

> Remember our brothers and sisters who have gone to their rest in the hope of rising again;
> Bring them and all the departed into the light of your presence.[141]

Specifically, it was the thought of Donal in the light of God's presence that brought a lump to my throat. As a family we had wrestled so long and hard with where our brother was – my sister had even asked at one point if he was in hell. It was shocking but it named the horror created by our fear and anger – that there was no meaning, just pointless destruction. Now, however, I could scarcely believe my eyes; what my heart had told me for a long time, that Donal was with God in the 'hope of the Resurrection', was now publicly proclaimed. Here at the end of the road I would hear those words proclaimed in solemn liturgy. I believed them with all my broken heart.

However, I was mightily relieved that I had not been given those words to read. I would never have been able to say them in the state I was in: tired, emotional and done-in, in all senses. The time came and I processed out onto the altar with the other priests; already the church was packed to the doors with pilgrims from over fifty countries, a sea of faces and colours.

The pilgrims who had received their *Compostela* (certificate) the day before had their countries of origin and their starting point announced at the Mass. It was an awesome vista of diversity, so many dreams and personal struggles, and the key need to acknowledge the journey through ritual and rite. I heard my nationality read out and my starting point – Hendaye on the French border. What a journey!

I went through the Mass in a blur of emotion and memory; Donal's T-shirt seemed heavy and conspicuous even though no one else could see it. I thought about all the Masses that Donal had attended; all the football games where he would have worn this shirt; all the smiles and words that I had heard him exchange over his 41 years. How much I had missed him, how my life had fallen apart when he went, and how I had struggled through these post-suicide years. I remembered one incident vividly that happened when we were young: he was hit by a stone on the head and it opened a bloody wound. I had been so powerless and unable to protect him – I wanted to be able to protect him now with this prayer. I hoped that this Santiago pilgrimage would finally lay all of this to rest, that this would be it. I was so tired of it all now.

I pulled myself together to do the Prayer of the Faithful, going down to the lectern with six other priests talking in other tongues. I was conscious that all the English speakers would be listening out in what was a sea of mainly Spanish. I began:

Through the intercession of St James, the great protector of pilgrims;
Make us strong in faith, and happy in hope, regardless of what comes.
May our pilgrim journey continue in our normal lives back home.
And sustain us so that we may finally reach the glory of God the Father.

Then there was a very erudite, long and wordy homily by the Dean that I could just about follow in Spanish. I lamented what a lost opportunity it was to say something meaning-ful to this huge largely secular gathering, who were then so receptive and with open hearts touched by the Road, many of whom would not darken the door of a church again. I so much wanted him to talk to people's experience of how they had been touched by Christ along the way. Then we were into the second part of the ceremony, the celebration of the Eucharist, where Jesus Christ offers his flesh and blood for the life of all. This spoke to me as never before: the very real suffering of Jesus in his humanity, the seeming triumph of evil on the cross, overcome by the self-giving love that expels all darkness.[142] The Camino was a small sharing in the suffering of Jesus, facing the darkness caused by suicide's reign, and rising through the light that is Christ. As the priest elevated the bread and the wine, I was very conscious of the great sacrifices I and all pilgrims had made on the road to be here – hunger, pain, suffering – partaking in some small way in Christ's great self-giving in the Mass.

Now that the consecration was over I knew that my prayer for the church and ministers was coming up fast. As I was seated right at the back of the sanctuary in the old choir stalls, I started to make my way down to the altar early. Then, to my horror, a Polish priest stepped out from the right and got to the altar before me to read 'my bit'. Reaching the altar, I paused behind him, unsure as to what to do next. When the Polish priest finished, the Dean motioned to me to step in and read the next section – the very one that I had not wanted to read. I think it was the element of surprise and not having time to prepare myself, but I was able to make it through those heart-breaking words, which were to be seared on my soul:

Remember our brothers and sisters who have gone to their rest in the hope of rising again;
Bring them and all the departed into the light of your presence.

As I returned to my seat I thought wryly that God has some sense of humour and that things do indeed happen for a reason, turning out much better than if we had planned them (the lesson of the Camino). I thought of the hope in those words, not just any hope but the hope of the Resurrection, to be with Christ in the light of his presence. This is what I had hoped for so long for Donal.[143] I had known it on an intellectual level but now I knew it within. As I made this powerful prayer, I felt like a prophet of old communicating God's message to an unbelieving world, a powerful witness for all who died through suicide: God will redeem them by raising them up. Taking off my alb in the sacristy afterwards, I felt this emotion wash through me, of relief and gratitude that the Camino was finally over and I could rest and recover.

Now that the Mass was over, I was really keen to see my Mexican friends, the Alvarez family who had carried me the last days, and also others whom I had met on the way. The huge 'Botafumeiro', the famous thurible used to bless pilgrims with incense (and disguise the bad odours emanating from many in the Middle Ages), did not make an appearance this time, disappointing many, and so the cathedral cleared out quite quickly. Outside in the constantly busy Plaza del Obradoiro, I quickly bumped into a number of familiar faces: the Belgian father of Mikael, the Dutch woman who had guided me to Güemes and Anuk from the Netherlands. There was the joy of meeting up again after absence, and of having shared significant moments along the way. They asked me about Donal's T-shirt and I proudly showed it off, bringing a tear to my eye. They had heard my voice over the sound system during the packed Pilgrim Mass; some had not realised I was a priest until then. We arranged to go out for a meal that night. However, I still couldn't find the Alvarez family, who had been so special for me in those last days, and I was saddened by this.

Even though it had been a great day, with lots of precious moments, I couldn't help thinking 'Is that it?' I thought there would be something more dramatic; in many ways it was a bit of an anticlimax. As I prepared to go out for the evening, it felt very strange not to be still earning my food on the road, wondering where I would sleep that night and always trying to 'get there'. Now that I had 'got there', it was quite flat, humdrum and ordinary – not at all what I thought it would be. That night the group of us who had walked together met for a celebration meal; looking around I knew that it was unlikely that we would meet again. We had shared some important moments though and shared a lot of our lives. Later we took to the quaint medieval streets of Santiago by night and gradually people drifted off to the rest of their lives.

Journey to the End of the Earth

'Well, that's it', I thought, closing the door of the Jesuit Community in Santiago behind me. The high from the Pilgrim Mass in the cathedral earlier that day was fading. I was looking forward to a quiet evening and a great sleep at last. This would be no ordinary sleep but the great healing slumber marathon that I craved. My head felt like the cockpit of a plane where all the warning lights were on: low fuel, equipment damaged, flying too low, wings fractured, urgently calling for an immediate landing.

In my mind I had already closed the door on the Camino experience and on the arduous, gruelling trip it had been. I just wanted time off now, away from the intensity, from the sheer physicality and especially from the unpredictable nature of what gets thrown at you. I felt like Ignatius returning home to Loyola to convalesce after being wounded at the Battle at Pamplona, craving a period of necessary recovery, restful healing and being protected from battles. I was in wind-down mode, already planning how I would quietly spend the final two days until my flight back to Ireland and also looking forward to normal life and what I had to do back home.

As I confidently breezed into the Jesuit dining room, I heard a familiar voice greet me in English. I was stunned, speechless. It took me a while to realise who it was – another Irish Jesuit friend of mine, Donal Godfrey,[144] who was based in the US. It turned out that he had been doing the *Camino Francés* from Sarria to Santiago (115 kilometres) over a week, finishing in Santiago the day before. Neither of us had realised we were on the same path, just one day apart, until our paths intersected at the Jesuit Community.

After the meal, we walked and talked, intuitively engaged in 'faith sharing' or spiritual conversation,[145] familiar to us both from Jesuit community life. I relished the chance to do this with a friend; it seemed the perfect ending to the Camino odyssey. I was horrified to hear of his encounter with bedbugs (common enough in the hostels) and the visible weal-like marks that they had left. I told him about my assorted medical problems and how I had just about scraped through.

Then Donal floated the idea that the next day we would go out together to Finisterre, which literally means 'the end of the world'. It was on the westernmost point of the coast and it was the unofficial end of the Camino. I found myself very torn, conscious of my much-desired sleep. Though I could feel the old pilgrim call stirring in the pit of my stomach, I pushed it down. After all, I had promised myself that I wouldn't do any more walking, would not endure any more painful challenges, and that it was just all rest and relaxation from here on. The idea of going to the place where the Camino met the ocean did not really appeal to me – 'I have done my Camino process and more than enough', I thought. 'The last thing I need is another trek.' I felt that I had finished what I had come to do, to deliver the T-shirt to Santiago, and that I had gotten everything I was going to get from the experience. My Jesuit training had taught me to avoid making quick decisions, however. Looking at the other side, there were some good things about going to Finisterre, obviously: the chance to spend more time with Donal, to do some more debriefing on the Camino, and to be in travel mode again, even if it was on the bus. It was to be Donal's last day before returning to the US also, so that was another factor in favour of going.

I knew what my body wanted here (R&R), but I knew that I needed to go through the Ignatian decision-making process of 'discernment'. Meaning to sift or to sort, discernment[146] is akin to the image of gold panning, where the gravel has to be shaken through a sieve to reveal the nuggets of precious metal. Essentially, it is separating the gold from the dross, the light from the dark, and the good from the bad in human experience. So, I put myself to discerning what the best thing to do was – asking myself what was God really wanting of me here and praying for freedom. On one level I knew what I wanted was to rest and to stay put, but this didn't feel quite right. Part of the problem, I realised, was that I found it very difficult to be free and detached, as Ignatius would have wanted. As I had promised myself this hard-earned rest and had looked forward to it so much during the last four weeks, I had become attached to it, and a little inflexible on it. I wasn't free anymore; I was chained to staying put.

These were some of the 'unfreedoms' and resistances that Ignatius mentions in his Rules for Discernment.[147] On one level it was understandable to crave rest after five weeks of tough exertion, but on another it was a lack of inner freedom – I would have plenty of time to rest when I got home and it really wasn't going to make much difference whether I went on the trip or not. However, I had a strange feeling that God wanted me to go on this trip for reasons that were not that clear to me. Still, I grumbled and moaned internally like a load-bearing Sherpa asked to make a push for a higher summit.[148] Finally, I said yes to Donal, and to the trip to the 'end of the world'; I felt lighter and more positive, confirmation of what I hoped would be a good decision.

So it was that we were on the early bus out of Santiago, heading due west for the Atlantic coast and the Cape of

Finisterre. Steeped in legend and myth, this place was believed to have been the westernmost point of the Iberian Peninsula (in fact, Cabo da Roca in Portugal is the most westerly). Made of hard crystalline rock, it plunges into the *Mare Tenebrosum* (or the 'dark sea', as the Atlantic was known). It sent a shiver down my back to know that the locals call it the 'Death Coast' (*Costa da Morte*) because of all the shipwrecks and fatalities that occurred there over many years. It sounded dramatic and almost dangerous. I had brought my backpack with me as I thought I might stay overnight and have time to reflect and rest.

I closed my eyes briefly on the two-hour coach journey and, not for the first time, thanked God for a safe arrival and for the end of an epic trip. The clouds rolled in as I looked out the window, and it began to rain. My first thought went to my fellow pilgrims who were out in this weather on their last three days' walk to the sea. As we careened along by coastal towns, beaches and rocky outcrops, it was very different to the inland Asturian Camino and bucolic meadows that I had walked.

Then I saw them – little isolated groups of hikers struggling against the wind in flapping capes, the rough broken trails and the tell-tale Camino markers with their distinctive yellow arrows. I felt a great love for these unknown people on their coastal pilgrim way, a pang of regret not to be walking, but mostly a sense of relief at being swept along at speed. I never realised how little I appreciated transport and technology. Now that I had walked so much, I knew what it meant.

We arrived into a wet and drizzly Finisterre and all romantic notions were dispelled, it being more like Limerick on a wet day. We sat in a fast-food café, surrounded by other dripping tourists, sipping hot chocolate and eating local sandwiches. We looked out on the persistent rain and low cloud over the harbour, which stripped it of any charm or beauty; I wondered whether I should have come. We were in danger of falling into a low mood and dull conversation, so we hurried out of the café and hit on the idea of walking the 4 kilometres out to the lighthouse on the cape. At least we would get to walk the last, ultimate section of the Camino where it met the wild Atlantic. So off we set, in a low, grey drizzle, for the cape at the end of the world.

This was a very short walk in comparison to what we had done to date, but it seemed interminable. The road continued to rise up into pine forests that seemed to draw down the clouds. To our left we could hear and smell the sea, but frustratingly it could not be seen. It was a real walk into the unknown, into a darkness of sorts, and a test of faith. I felt distinctly uneasy and a bit troubled. One of the books that I had found on my brother Donal's bedside table after his death was *The Cloud of Unknowing*.[149] The key insight of this book was that God could not be known by knowledge or intellect but rather through a 'dart of longing love' from the heart. In many ways my post-suicide life had taken on this aspect of not knowing what lay ahead, not being able to see clearly and having to blindly trust. 'Here I am again', I thought, grimly trudging up an endless hill into the mist, not feeling much love in my heart and having misgivings as to whether it was worth it. Again, the dogged determination of my fellow Jesuit, Donal, kept me going.

Things started to appear out of the mist: first, several hikers, then a statue of a female pilgrim clutching a bunch of flowers beside the road. It seemed unbearably sad in the swirling mist, somewhat funereal; I shuddered at the thought. Then we came across a *rollo*, a medieval stone cross, embedded in a platform of rock. With the billowing mist and in the half-light this looked decidedly macabre and we took some dramatic photos. Suddenly, we came upon some small shops and then a small café with people huddled inside, and finally a huge grim white and brown building emerged from the mist. This low squat building operated as a hotel, while an octagonal granite lighthouse was located behind it. As we moved on out onto the rocky point behind the lighthouse, many metres above the Atlantic, we saw figures moving about on the headland in the mist, with small fires billowing smoke at their feet. This seemed to be the height of bizarreness in what had been a strange day. They were pilgrims engaged in a peculiar ritual of burning their clothes at the end of the Camino. Enwrapped within a certain cathartic intensity, this scene made riveting watching, despite the acrid smoke. Nonetheless, it felt like we were intruding on their privacy and we retreated, having no business there.

As we turned around to go home in the rain, a certain idea slowly but insistently imposed itself on my consciousness: 'There is an item of clothing I have to burn and now I understand why I am here and the significance of this seemingly wasted day.' It was a terrifying idea in some ways as I grasped the import of it and what it would cost me. To burn Donal's T-shirt, the last connection I had to him in this world, and to let go totally of my grasp on him. But I could not deny this little moment of revelation and the clarity with which it appeared to me as being a sound idea, an idea from God. Ignatius defined consolation, the movement towards the light, as 'any increase of our faith, our hope, and our love. A deep-down peace comes in just our living life as "being in our Father's house".'[150] It seemed to me that this was what I was experiencing now, this sense of great peace, even amid the feelings of fear and loss.

This deeper sense of calm, quiet self-possession and interior joy was to last all day. When I explained my idea to my friend Donal he was very supportive of it, though he had to go back that evening. Saying goodbye to him was not easy at this point; I was alone with my conflicting emotions. I booked a cheap room in Finisterre, precariously located on the top floor of an impossibly narrow house with steep steps, but with a wide panoramic view over the harbour. I could see many fishing boats tied up below, though Monte Pindo across the bay was obscured by cloud. That evening I visited the castle of San Carlos, perched on a rocky promontory, and, though there was a great tour guide, I couldn't concentrate or fix on anything. Even though there were other pilgrims I knew in town, I decided to eat alone in the guest house, and gather my courage for what I knew would be a difficult day.

I awoke at 6.30 a.m. with the light penetrating the flimsy curtains. It was a bright, clear morning in Finisterre on the Atlantic coast. The turquoise dawn that greeted my tired eyes was in such contrast to the drizzle and mist of the previous day. I missed my friend Donal, who had gone back to Santiago to catch his flight, and I felt very much on my own in this unknown territory, the Camino beyond the Camino. Fixed in my head was what I knew I had to do from having observed other pilgrims engage in their bizarre clothes-burning ritual the day before. The finality of it was terrifying.

I lifted my rucksack as I had done countless times in the last 40 days, except this time it was strangely light; there was only one item of clothing in it, a Barcelona FC T-shirt. Placing it inside, I had an image of my brother Donal playing football, happy and well. It hurt to remember. My rucksack seemed a fitting way to transport this precious garment to its final resting place. I left at 7.30 a.m. on a fasting stomach, nothing new for me, but somehow it felt more important here.[151] There was so much I desired: to be forgiven, a release from guilt, from grief, and, for my brother Donal especially, peace of body and soul for him. There were no other pilgrims on the road, unlike the previous day when there had been many. I marvelled at the continually evolving sunrise in its interplay with the clouds. I dreaded what lay ahead, yet felt impelled to carry it out. I prayed for strength.

On the way up the hill I passed the church of Santa María das Areas, a twelfth-century Romanesque church, which we had visited the previous day. I had their prayer card in my hand with a graphic image of the suffering Christ figure by an unknown fourteenth-century sculptor. It vividly portrays his last moments before death. A super realistic portrayal of pain and agony, it could have been gruesome and macabre

– if it were the end – and yet it was a symbol of hope and strength for me now.

Strengthened by this I pressed on towards the lighthouse on the cape, this far-flung finger of land thrust into the Atlantic. It was as dramatic a place as I have ever seen, all the more poignant for the ritual I was about to perform. I got to the end of the path behind the lighthouse and started off down the rough path among the scorched rocks, marked by other pilgrim offerings. Then I suddenly realised that I didn't have any matches or a lighter. I had presumed that the little shop back up the road would be open, but of course it wasn't at this hour. I was shocked. I stared out to sea disconsolate, making out distant whitecaps. 'What a stupid mistake', I thought, 'that such a simple thing would sink my whole plan.'

After a few moments I heard a noise behind me and saw another hiker making his way through the rocks. He was French but we communicated easily, a non-verbal intuition that understands the important nature of what has to be done. He lent me his lighter and then discreetly moved away to give me space.

I held the T-shirt for a moment, torn within, as this was the last fragment of Donal that I possessed. This would be it, no more. There was a terrible finality about it and I knew well what this sacred rite was: a letting go of my brother, of my grief, and of the traumatic last few years that had been so terrible. There was something comforting about my grief, my pain, and my hold on Donal, which I was putting in jeopardy here. It was easier to live in the dusty, memory-filled rooms of the past than to open up to new air and new life. I had identified myself with my mourning for so long, it had become part of who I was. The idea of losing this security and comfort blanket was terrifying.

I wanted to stop, to go home, to flee, but at a deeper level I knew that I was bound to carry out this ritual of fire. It was trusting in a future of hope, and critically in my belief that I would see my dear Donal again. I wouldn't need any earthly reminders of him as we would be having a face-to-face encounter in heaven. Though tempted to flee, I knew not to reverse the decision I had made to come initially.[152] It was an enormous act of will to put the flame to the Barcelona FC T-shirt that I had carried all the way from the French border, some 800 kilometres away.

And then, the anti-climax – it wouldn't light! The material was too heavy and the wind was too strong. I tried a more sheltered spot between two rocks but to no avail. I looked up to see where my French Good Samaritan was, but he was nowhere to be seen; I was worried about using up all his lighter fluid.

Eventually I hit on the idea of using a tissue as a crude tinder to get the T-shirt burning. Fortunately it worked and within seconds I had a steady flame from the tissue that created enough heat to melt the heavy fabric. Because melt is what it did, turning into globules of molten fabric, spilling onto the ground. It happened so rapidly, not what I was expecting. Disappearing before my eyes, I wanted to hold onto the last familiar remnants. I was alarmed at how quickly it all broke down and disintegrated.

Suddenly, unable to hold the shirt any longer, I let it fall into a fiery heap. I felt myself disintegrating. I fell into sobs beside a nearby rock, in a foetal position for the emotional meltdown that I was experiencing. It hurt intensely; these were wracking sobs that came from the bottom of my soul – all that grief, all that anger, all that loss, all that pain, everything that had nowhere to go, now it all came out into the Iberian light. This really was the end of the road, the desperate plea of an exhausted pilgrim unable to bear the load. The black scorched rocks and remnants of burnt clothing everywhere seemed a fitting environment for this purging of the past – a veritable wasteland of memory and bitter regrets. I had been drinking from a terribly bitter cup, brought to my knees with suffering. Once the spasms came to a natural end I dusted myself down, feeling empty and creased. I was barely able to stand and struggled to believe that some of the darkness had passed and that some new hope had been born.

Afterwards I went and sat in the sun with my empty rucksack. Gradually, I began to feel well despite the ordeal I had been through. A fellow pilgrim kindly agreed to take my photo and it reveals a face aglow, at peace and transformed. I sat there for a long time, just being. It was God's time now, *kairos* time, outside of chronological time, when extraordinary things happen. This experience of living in God's love freely given was deeply consoling and satisfying.[153] I had a strong sense of that 'giftedness', grace or blessing as I had not earned or deserved this in any way. I felt the whole journey on the Camino had been a preparation for this moment, a stripping down of the ego and self-centredness, and a being open to providence and what the moment brought. This was the greatest gift that I could have hoped for, totally unexpected, literally at the last moment, and all the more welcome for that.

On the way back to Finisterre I spied a rare sandy beach down at the bottom of the endless cliffs; I made my way down some steps and changed. The plunge into the green surf of the Atlantic took my breath away. The cold sent a tingle through my synapses and I felt new life surge within me. A few strokes out into the Bay of Biscay and the years and the tears fell away – it felt like I was born again. I thrashed the salty brine with my fists for pure joy. Back on the beach I found a standpipe where I could wash off the salt. Ignatius once said that God showers down gifts and blessings on us like a waterfall. As I washed, it struck me that all I have and all that I am have been given to me, and particularly the Camino has been God's gift, custom-designed for me.

Undeniably the Spirit was speaking to me directly. The message was stop trying to go it alone with your own striving and solo efforts; lay back and trust God, trust the universe and the road to deliver to you what you need.

I could see now the invitation to get off the mad wheel of competitiveness and busyness that the world promotes.

I knew the importance of walking my own Camino at my own pace. This meant not being distracted by others, keeping my own quiet and humble goals. I understood I would get there in God's time and through God's love, by trusting and following the urgings within. I knew in my bones that God works through all things, people, circumstances and events, to indicate God's love for me. It is only through my response of gratitude, humility and love that life can be lived authentically.

On the bus going back to Santiago, my heart fairly sang. The Galician countryside was dazzling in the afternoon sun, such a contrast to the bleak drizzle of the day before. I marvelled at how a life can change during one itinerant month or even one dramatic day on the coast. I could feel God's love for me made tangible in these last hours particularly, on the enlightening Camino and also during my whole life. In the light of this radiance, I prayed for forgiveness for all the mistakes, for the courage to press on into whatever new life God had in store for me. Like Ignatius did at one key moment, I was asking, 'What kind of a new life is this that we are now beginning?'[154] For the first time in a long time I had real hope.

On arriving in Santiago again, I was content to amble around the old town, to be in the cathedral and to catch up with some friends. Just before I left for home, the Jesuit superior, Father Amor, told me 'I think you really got the Camino thing'; I had to agree with him, although I rather think that *it* got *me*. Walking the road to Santiago had stripped me of my illusions and prepared me for a new awakening.

It was a considerably leaner, lighter and transformed person who finally arrived in Galway on a lovely July evening. I walked with my friends through the Spanish Arch, appropriately enough, and they accompanied me the last few hundred yards to my home. After some customary tea and scones and a lot of talk, eventually I made it to my own room. Collapsing into bed, I was in heaven.

Epilogue

There is a saying in Santiago that if you walk five times around the cathedral you will meet all your friends from the Camino. I was particularly keen to meet the Alvarez family, who I feared might have left Spain at this point, but also all the many others I had met along the way. The day after I arrived back from Finisterre, I made my last visit to the cathedral. I didn't even have to walk once around it. No sooner had I left the Jesuit residence in Santiago than I ran into a couple of my former students from the school where I was chaplain. They had just finished the Camino too, a few days behind me, and there was lots of catching up to be done.

Later that day, I popped into the busy cathedral for a quick goodbye prayer and was delighted to meet my friends from Tineo, the 80-year-old Frenchman Anton and his Belgian helper, Frederick. I talked animatedly with Frederick for a few moments in the aisle, but Anton, whom I joined in the pews, said nothing but just embraced me warmly and held my gaze for what seemed an eternity. Even without a common language, this was a beautiful moment of communion that only shared experience on the Road can give.

Outside the cathedral on a side street I ran into a jubilant Sarah, who had just finished the Camino. She proudly showed me the new boots that she had gotten the day after I left her in Lugo. She hugged me warmly and introduced me to a Dutch friend as 'the guy who saved me'. It did me much

good to see her so well and on the other side of so many
difficulties.

Just when I thought I couldn't bear any more of this emotional intensity, and time was pressing, I ran into a familiar
group of Latino faces at the north gate. I was thrilled to meet
again the Alvarez family from Mexico on their way to the
airport. They greeted me so warmly and I felt so strongly
like they were family that I was in tears. I was trying to find
the words to thank them in Spanish but they shortcut this
attempt by presenting me with a very Mexican thing, a card
called a *ramillete espiritual* (spiritual bouquet), which outlined
all the prayers, penances and Masses they would offer for me.
Once again, their generosity overtook my attempts to thank
them. I was reduced to an incoherent, blubbering wreck; I do
believe it was one of the best presents I ever received.

Back at the Jesuit residence, I packed my tired-looking
hiking gear. Unfortunately, I wasn't able to take my faithful
yellow backpack as cabin baggage, so I tenderly placed it in
the storeroom for recycling. It had served me well and hopefully it would serve someone else well too – another lesson in
detachment. As the plane took off from Santiago airport, the
Camino was laid out below and I felt that I had left a huge
weight back there too. I prayed that this new life before me,
whatever it was, would be lived like a pilgrim, reflective and
filled with gratitude.

On the final bus journey back home to Galway, I savoured
the lush Irish landscape as if arriving for the first time; I was
tingling with the delicious anticipation of homecoming.
Walking from the bus station I felt like I was on another leg of
the Camino, focused on passing through the city, as people
brushed past with their cares and concerns. However, I felt
an enormous sense of joy and contentment in simply being
alive. A small number of Jesuits, friends and family gathered to meet me, appropriately enough, at the Spanish Arch
on the banks of the River Corrib in Galway. I fell into their
embraces and affection, the returning pilgrim but hardly a

hero. I solemnly placed a scallop shell around their necks, a small ritual of inclusion in the Camino journey that would be theirs to walk one day. We walked the last few hundred metres together to the Jesuit house. I was home at last. Getting into my own bed never did feel so delicious and luxurious as it did for that magnificent and much-anticipated sleep.

The next morning, I went for a walk on the Salthill promenade and met an old friend of mine. I was still full of enthusiasm and bonhomie on the homecoming high. 'I did the Camino!' I proudly proclaimed.

'Did you walk all of it?'

'Well, I had to take the bus a few times, but that wasn't actually the important thing ...' I answered, gearing up to share my many and varied insights.

To my dismay, he cut me off: 'Oh now', he said, 'You know Michael from Spiddal; he is over 60 and he walked the whole thing last year.' It was a none-too-subtle putdown. It came as a shock to me to realise that this was the end of the conversation. The competition ethos runs deep and wide, I realised, not only on the trail, but in the heart of ordinary life. I felt like I had been judged and had come up wanting; it left me frustrated and disappointed and the conversation petered out.

As I sat on my own later, overlooking the bay, I ruefully remembered that I had had a lot of preparation for this. I could see both Ignatius and Donal laughing at the irony of the situation. The whole point of the exercise was to become free of people's expectations or approval and here I was caught again. Very soon, I felt my resistance thaw out and I began to laugh with them. 'The learning never stops', I thought. At that the sun came out from behind a cloud and the waters of Galway Bay glistened in response.

I reflected that the core message for me was to be grateful for all that I had received and not to compare myself to anyone else. A Jesuit friend of mine used to say 'compare and despair'. It looked like I was going to need some more time on the road with this one. With that I took up my bag and faced into the westerly breeze, seeing the flinty shine of the Burren across from me. I knew then that few would understand what had happened on that long month in Spain; I didn't even know how I would begin to communicate it. I resolved to let it mature within me until the time was right; this book is the fruit of that process.

Endnotes

Chapter I

1   Donal, from the Irish word *Domhnall*, means 'world mighty'. Donal is its anglicised form. It was the ninth most popular name in early Ireland (Donnchadh O'Corrain and Fidelma Maguire, *Gaelic Personal Names* (Dublin: The Academy Press, 1981)).

2   Joseph Tylenda, *A Pilgrim's Journey: The Autobiography of Ignatius of Loyola* (Collegeville, MN: The Order of St Benedict, 1991), No. 8, pp. 14–15. The emphasis is my own.

3   Michael Ivens (edited by Joseph Munitiz), *An Approach to Saint Ignatius of Loyola* (Oxford: Way Books, 2008), pp. 8–9.

4   It was intriguing the way that Ignatius found the spirit within his affectivity or feelings; he had to have time out, recuperation and solitude in order for these to surface (see Michael O'Sullivan, 'Trust Your Feelings but Use Your Head: Discernment and the Psychology of Decision Making', *Studies in the Spirituality of Jesuits*, Vol. 22, No. 4, 1990.)

5   References to the Spiritual Exercises are based on David L. Fleming, *Draw Me into Your Friendship – The Spiritual Exercises: A Literal Translation and a Contemporary Reading of the Spiritual Exercises* (St Louis, MO: Institute of Jesuit Sources, 1996). The abbreviation 'SpEx' is used throughout this book as an abbreviation for the Spiritual Exercises.

6   Described in Brendan McManus, 'Ignatian Pilgrimage: The Inner Journey – Loyola to Manresa on Foot', *The Way*, Vol. 49, No. 3, July 2010.

7   A bereaved father (played by Martin Sheen) decides to walk the Way of St James in honour of his son (www.theway-themovie.com).

8   Margaret Silf, *Inner Compass: An Invitation to Ignatian Spirituality* (Chicago, IL: Loyola Press, 1998), p. 119.

9   Surprisingly, Ignatius encouraged great desires; the idea was that God is in our deepest desires and not in superficial ones. Pilgrimage and journeying allows us to go deeper so that we distinguish what is valuable for us and what is dross (see Silf, *Inner Compass*, Chapter 8).

10 That is, as a seeker or wanderer. It means cutting ties and leaving home, leaving the past behind, to be open to something new and hopefully enlightening. 'Outwardly becoming a wandering and unknown stranger and inwardly, on the unknown road towards one's true self, towards God' (Peter Muller and Angel Fernandez de Aranguiz (translated by Laurie Dennett), *Every Pilgrim's Guide to Walking to Santiago de Compostela* (Norwich: Canterbury Press, 2010), pp. xxv).

11 Ignatius reflected his self-understanding when he referred to himself as 'the pilgrim' in relating his life story. See *A Pilgrim's Journey*, p. xiv.

12 It is very sobering to realise that backpack weight is the key criteria for injury-free walking, and that 10 per cent of your body weight is the ideal. Inevitably, compromises have to be made and this radical one cost a few nights' sleep but was probably worth it overall (see www.urcamino.com/camino-frances/what-to-carry).

13 Dockside poem in Hondarribia, Gipuzkoa, Basque Country; my translation.

14 *Camino* translates as 'way' in English, which seems to capture my search for closure and a reconfiguration of faith. Early Christians also described themselves as following 'the Way' in the Acts of the Apostles.

15 Also known as the Examen of Consciousness, this prayer is a key one in Ignatius' Spiritual Exercises (SpEx 43) because it helps process the day and reflect on where the Spirit has been in your daily life (see www.loyolapress.com/how-can-i-pray-try-the-daily-examen.htm).

Chapter 2

16 I couldn't help but think of the Gospel of John, 15: 1–17, where Jesus is the true vine and God is the gardener who prunes the branches for greater fruitfulness.

17 One of the Spiritual Exercises has you imagine that you are selected by a great king or leader to be part of their team, which means giving up all luxuries and selfishness in order to be part of the world-changing divine vision (SpEx 91–100).

18 This is simply a being aware state of mindfulness, being present to your body and the moment (see http://goodlifezen.com/zen-and-the-art-of-walking).

19 Loyola is also the starting point for the Ignatian walking pilgrimage, the *Camino Ignaciano*, which I had done 20 years previously (see http://caminoignaciano.org/en).

20 Discernment is '… an inner compass that shows each of us the path of intimacy with God' (Monty Williams, *The Gift of Spiritual Intimacy* (Toronto, ON: Novalis, 2009), p. 28).

21 A 'spiritual exercise' is awareness, meditation or reflection, any practice which helps to increase openness to the Spirit (SpEx 1).

22 Fleming, *Draw Me Into Your Friendship*, p. 5.

23 This is the theological belief that nothing is beyond the healing love of Christ.

24 Detachment is freedom from addictive or damaging dependences (Silf, *Inner Compass*, pp. 141–169).

25 I wanted to live the Ignatian ideal of leadership through self-awareness and self-reflection, staying true to one's own values and principles through being 'detached' or 'indifferent', despite what others are doing (Chris Lowney, *Heroic Leadership* (Chicago, IL: Loyola Press, 2003), pp. 27–31).

26 The name comes from the Sanskrit word for god or deity.

27 Originally I thought that I would be swimming every day on this coastal route but this was to be the only one.

28 We belong to God and other things come second, otherwise they can get in the way, disturb our 'balance' and make us slaves to them, e.g. addictions (SpEx 23).

29 Matthew 5: 14; the light has to shine unobstructed in order to see the way.

30 Ignatius invites us to face our fears, make discerned decisions and act against unhealthy attachments to achieve genuine freedom (SpEx 149–155).

31 Eric Walker and Chris Lennie, *Los Caminos del Norte, A: Ruta de la Costa, 1: Irún–Villaviciosa* (London: The Confraternity of Saint James, 2010).

Chapter 3

32 NLP is an alternative therapy for the treatment of all sorts of psychological and physical problems.

33 Intent on killing a 'Moor' whom he saw as having insulted Our Lady, Ignatius could not decide what to do and so dropped the reins to let the mule he was riding decide. Fortunately his mule took another path to that of the Moor. This divesting himself of responsibility was clearly not discernment but probably drove him to find a better way of making decisions subsequently.

34 It is crucial to identify those compulsions or negative attachments that stop us being free (SpEx 15 and 179).

35 The insight is 'give up control, let go' (see http://ignatianeducator.com/tag/xavier/).

36 In the Spiritual Exercises Ignatius suggests that you ask directly for the 'grace' or desire that you seek (SpEx 48).

37 This is the quintessential Camino greeting, meaning 'Have a great walk.'

38 The irony was that Ignatius's devastating injury was to his leg also, and he always walked with a limp after that. It was this physical injury and being forced to recuperate that facilitated his conversion.

39 Reflectively reviewing the events of the day reveals another layer of meaning (SpEx 43).

[40] In the fundamental Exercise, the Principle and Foundation (SpEx 23), Ignatius has a curious phrase that we should not 'prefer health to sickness'. He lists it under things relating to indifference or detachment (being free of), but it is challenging to be able to accept illness freely, or accept that it could be part of a divine plan.

Chapter 4

[41] One of Ignatius' particularly useful guidelines for decisions is never to go back on a decision that was well made, when you were in consolation (i.e. when in good shape, balanced and free of influences) (SpEx 318).

[42] Flowing from the Exercises is the technique of Spiritual Direction, actively listening to help the other find freedom to choose well (see William A. Barry and William J. Connolly, *The Practice of Spiritual Direction* (New York: Seabury Press, 1982), pp. 3–12).

[43] He was the illustrator for a Spanish book on the Jesuits: www.salterrae.es/catalogo/pdf/En_compania_de_Jesus.pdf.

[44] The Spiritual Exercises are normally done in a retreat house, a secluded setting, but Ignatius does make provision for adapting them to different situations; the Camino would be an obvious one (SpEx Annotations 18 and 20).

[45] Intriguingly, we are told, 'The greatest consolation he experienced was gazing at the sky and the stars' (*A Pilgrim's Journey*, p. 17).

[46] Ever the pragmatist, Ignatius has us consider the pros and cons of a decision, especially seeing it from the opposite point of view to our own (SpEx 181).

[47] Adios literally means 'to God'. It is an abbreviation of 'A Dios vais' ('You're going to God', meaning to the Kingdom of Heaven).

[48] Ignatius would have understood freedom as 'freedom for' living life fully and 'freedom from' unhealthy attachments, such as compulsions or addictions.

[49] 'Heart burning within me' is a reference to the disciples listening to Jesus on the road to Emmaus, but it captures a particularly Jesuit way of praying (see Michael Harter (ed.), *Hearts on Fire: Praying with Jesuits* (Chicago, IL: Loyola Press, 2005)).

[50] Echoing the Suscipe, a prayer of great affection and gratitude at the end of the Exercises (SpEx 234).

Chapter 5

[51] Ignatian freedom is to accept freely any conditions or circumstances as a gift without being limited by preconceptions (SpEx 21).

[52] Ignatius advocated putting the best interpretation on people and treating them kindly (SpEx Annotation 22).

53 The voluntary body *Asociaciones de Amigos del Camino de Santiago* provides hospitality in many hostels (www.caminosantiago.org/cpperegrino/comun/inicio.asp).

54 This is classic desolation – dissonant feelings that lead one away from God (SpEx 317).

55 '... try to be like a balance at equilibrium, without leaning to either side' (SpEx 179).

56 Joseph Munitiz, 'St Ignatius of Loyola and Severe Depression', *The Way*, Vol. 44, No. 3, July 2005, pp. 58–59.

57 A good idea taken to excess distorts and becomes the opposite (SpEx 332).

58 Ignatius had a section of the Spiritual Exercises called 'Rules for Discernment', which were practical distilled guidelines on decision making derived from his own experiences (SpEx 313–336).

59 The bad spirit is disguised as an angel of light to deceive the good person (SpEx 332).

60 We need to examine the whole sequence of thoughts to see where they soured (SpEx 333 and 334).

61 Gerard O'Mahony uses the image of a boat having to continually adjust while crossing a tidal estuary to illustrate balance in moods (Gerard O'Mahony, *Finding the Still Point* (Guilford: Eagle Publishing, 1992)).

Chapter 6

62 Seeing everything as a gift comes from realising how much I have received and opens my heart (SpEx 233).

63 Camino hostels are also known as *refugios*, from the Latin *refugium*, meaning 'refuge' or 'shelter'. The name is seen as an allusion to Nuestra Señora del Refugio, or Our Lady of Refuge, one of the names for the Virgin Mary in the Christian tradition.

64 Seeking to cultivate an 'attitude of gratitude' (Brian J. Lehane, 'Attitude of Gratitude: The Examen Prayer of St. Ignatius', *Partners*, www.jesuits-chgdet.org/wp-content/uploads/2011/03/Partners_FA09.Sprituality.pdf) (SpEx 32–43).

65 From an Ignatian point of view, caught at an existential low point, I was being pulled by different 'spirits' and struggling to stay faithful to the rules of discernment (SpEx 316–336).

66 This was an experience of consolation, a 'deep down peace' and trusting attitude (SpEx 316).

67 This is the key Ignatian question of meaning, but it probably betrays some frustration and desolation here, i.e. temptations to despair, undermining the decision made and giving up (SpEx 317).

68 Knowing I was in need, I asked for the strength and patience to get me through (SpEx 48).

69 Brendan McManus, 'Surviving Suicide', *The Furrow*, Vol. 61, No. 2, February 2010, pp. 98–108.

70 This is better known by its Latin title, *agere contra*, a form of Ignatian asceticism necessary for spiritual progress. Ivens outlines well the priority of finding a mean or balance (Michael Ivens, *Understanding the Spiritual Exercises* (Leominster: Gracewing, 1998)) (SpEx 13, 317, 322).

71 The enforced time out allowed many issues and stumbling blocks to arise and be addressed in prayer, freeing me to move onwards on my journey (see Carol A. Smith and Eugene F. Merz, *Moment by Moment: A Retreat in Everyday Life* (Notre Dame, IN: Ave Maria Press, 2005)).

Chapter 7

72 The ideal of walking the perfect Camino with no deviations, doctors or assistance.

73 I realised that I was being unfairly attacked and unreflectively responding in kind; instead, I knew that I had to act against this (SpEx 13) to restore my peace, balance and goodwill towards her.

74 Ignatius has this image about ourselves as a military fortress and that we are attacked by the enemy at the weakest point, where defenses are low. For me it was the guilt trip about not walking a 'perfect' Camino. An impenetrable fortress seemed to me the best defense against this aggressive 'enemy' (SpEx 327).

75 Following the *humble* Christ means moderating one's interior thoughts and feelings to avoid being a victim of anger or the ego, but rather trying to explore alternative ways of dialogue and resolution (Tad Dunne, 'Extremism in Ignatius of Loyola', *Review for Religious*, Vol. 45, No. 3, May–June 1986, pp. 345–355).

76 Walking is one way of reflecting on experience and finding God (SpEx 77).

77 Joyce Rupp, *Walk in a Relaxed Manner: Life Lessons from the Camino* (Maryknoll, NY: Orbis Books, 2005).

78 This enigmatic phrase from Luke's Gospel sums up the personal nature of Ignatian prayer.

Chapter 8

79 Joseph Munitiz, 'St Ignatius of Loyola and Severe Depression', p. 69.

80 In times of desolation, people are led by the evil one, who guides and counsels falsely. People are tempted to give up on a positive outlook and adopt deceptive thoughts as their own (SpEx 318).

81 In the Principle and Foundation of Spiritual Exercise 23, Ignatius says that we must hold ourselves indifferent or in balance, to be free to make wise and prudent choices.

82 The Sacred Heart of Jesus is an old devotion, dating from around the seventeenth century, of love for the heart of Jesus, the living, loving person of Christ. It is centred on the heart of Jesus as the symbol of divine love.

[83] 'Nothing can separate us from the love of God' (Romans 8: 39) was proclaimed on Donal's memorial card.

[84] Ignatius recommended removing yourself from distractions and noise so as to better listen to God's voice (20th Annotation, SpEx 20).

[85] Mark 15: 34 – in an extraordinary moment of humanity Jesus quotes Psalm 22: 'My God, my God, why have you forsaken me?'

[86] Harold S. Kushner, *When Bad Things Happen to Good People* (New York: Anchor Books, 2004).

[87] Sometimes prayer is not enough and you have to do something concrete and challenging to break out of a rut (Paul Valadier, 'Pray as if Everything Depends on You, Act as if Everything Depends on God', *Orientations for Spiritual Growth*, www.jesuits.ca/orientations/hevenesi.pdf).

[88] Console is an Irish registered charity supporting and helping people bereaved through suicide by means of support groups, counselling and prevention programmes (www.console.ie).

[89] Good can come out of terrible grief or disasters, but God didn't intend or engineer this to happen (Richard Leonard, *Where the Hell Is God?* (Mahwah, NJ: Paulist Press, 2010)).

Chapter 9

[90] It is impossible to know how many people have to drop out along the way, but anecdotally it seems a high percentage (see www.caminodesantiago.me/community/threads/dropout-rate.6799).

[91] How we use something determines if it brings us away from or closer to God (www.ignatianspirituality.com/ignatian-prayer/the-spiritual-exercises/ignatius-three-part-vision).

[92] A key part of the Spiritual Exercises are the 'Rules for Discernment' (SpEx 313–336), which encapsulate Ignatius' wisdom on dealing with moods and impulses. Some are so practical that I refer to them as rules of thumb; the one that applies here (318) is don't let changeable feelings dictate your actions, rather stick to good decisions and sound rationales when making decisions (Michael O'Sullivan, 'Trust Your Feelings, But Use Your Head', p. 21).

[93] The central character in *The Shack*, Mack, uses this phrase to talk about his grief following the death of his beloved daughter, Missy, and how he confronts God with this particular anger and resentment. This was something close to my own story that I could relate to (William Paul Young, *The Shack: Where Tragedy Confronts Eternity* (Los Angeles, CA: Windblown Media, 2007)).

[94] This line echoes directly the words and structure that Ignatius used to describe one of his first spiritual insights where he uses reflection and interior examination to notice what's happening within him (*A Pilgrim's Journey*, p. 14).

95   Mark Williams and Danny Penman, *Mindfulness: Finding Peace in a Frantic World* (New York: Rodale Books, 2011).

96   This is the essence of Anthony DeMello's teaching on awareness and 'waking up' (www.demellospirituality.com/awareness/37.html).

97   Andy Otto, 'The Ignatian Way: Contemplative in Action', *God in All Things*, 19 July 2012, http://godinallthings.com/2012/07/19/the-ignatian-way-contemplative-in-action.

98   In Greek there are two words for time, *chronos* and *kairos*. *Chronos* refers to chronological or regimented 'clock' time, while *kairos* means 'out of time' or the 'opportune time'. It has a spiritual sense to it: time that is removed from the business of life, where the value of just being dominates.

99   Ignatius had a rule of thumb that when you are in doubt about someone or their motives, it is advisable to put the best interpretation on them, to give them the benefit of the doubt (SpEx 22).

Chapter 10

100 www.theway-themovie.com, with Martin Sheen. I saw this as preparation before I left, but didn't understand it until my return.

101 Steve Bevans, 'God Is a Verb', *Catholic Theological Union*, October 2010, www.ctu.edu/word-ctu/article/god-verb.

102 David Lonsdale, *Dance to the Music of the Spirit: The Art of Discernment* (London: Darton, Longman and Todd, 1992).

103 For example, Luke 24: 36 and John 14: 27.

104 The word 'Eucharist' means 'thanksgiving'.

Chapter 11

105 The paradox of a beauty that threatens; from William Butler Yeats' poem 'Easter, 1916'.

106 This same tension of being at the limits is evident in Jesus' statement on the cross, 'My God, My God, why have you forsaken me?' (Matthew 27: 45), which I often repeated to myself on the road.

107 The name of a Van Morrison song, meaning to face into hardship, to take the hard road, not having much choice.

108 Ignatius would call this the work of the destructive 'bad spirit', planting doubts, lowering the mood and raising obstacles to block progress (SpEx 315).

109 At 1146 metres, it is higher than any Irish mountain.

110 Gratitude is key to the Examen prayer, realising how much we are loved.

111 The point is that this is a movement away from God, and needs to be remedied by acting against it (SpEx 319).

112 Although the scale is obviously different in my brother's case, it is still the examination of moods that is a valid subject matter for discernment (see O'Mahony, *Finding the Still Point*, pp. 19–32).

113 Don't go back on good decisions made when you were in a free and balanced state (SpEx 318) (see also Thomas H. Green, *Weeds Among the Wheat* (Notre Dame, IN: Ave Maria Press, 1984), pp. 107–111).

114 On a thirty-day pilgrimage across Spain in 1994 I had a similar crisis moment where, having run out of food, I realised that I couldn't do it on my own and had to ask God to help me; that made all the difference.

Chapter 12

115 Luke 23: 46.

116 http://caminodesantiago.consumer.es/etapa-de-tineo-a-pola-de-allande (the 2011 app version).

117 Joseph Tetlow, *Ignatius Loyola: Spiritual Exercises* (New York: Crossroad, 1992), p. 54.

118 Walking the last 100 kilometres is the minimum requirement to get the official certificate, the *Compostela*.

119 Ignatius was very much a person of extremes in the early stages of his spiritual life at Manresa; at one stage he even cut a hole in his shoes in order to suffer more while walking. Later he realised the folly of this and how much damage he had done to his health. He learned to be much more discerning, prudent and balanced in decision making (*A Pilgrim's Journey*, Chapter 3).

120 Brendan McManus, 'Surviving Suicide'.

121 I was grateful for this critical service to me; I needed to face up to the realities of what was coming up and, importantly, what my options were. It wasn't good enough just to drift along and stumble into choices; I needed to decide what my priorities were.

122 The image of an inner fire is central to Ignatius' idea of discernment: 'Spiritual consolation is an experience of being so on fire with God's love', 'The soul comes to be inflamed with love of its Creator and Lord' (SpEx 316).

123 One refreshing thing about the Camino is that people rarely ask you about or define you in terms of what job or role you have; rather it is about who you are and how you relate.

124 Matthew 5: 5–8.

125 It was in the sense of being Nouwen's wounded healer that the trauma I had been through, far from being a block, could be of help for others (see Henri Nouwen, *The Wounded Healer: Ministry in Contemporary Society* (New York: Doubleday, 1972)).

Chapter 13

126 SpEx 319.

127 The Spanish name Consuelo is translated as 'solace', 'hope' or 'consolation' and is linked to the Virgin Mary's title 'Nuestra Señora del Consuelo', i.e. Our Lady of Consolation.

[128] Michael Harter (ed.) *Hearts on Fire*, p. 119.

[129] James Martin, *The Jesuit Guide to (Almost) Everything* (New York: HarperOne, 2010), p. 264.

Chapter 14

[130] Reading Tolkien's *The Lord of the Rings* as a teenager had made a deep impression on me, particularly how the epic struggle for good versus evil comes down to the deliberate actions of a few heroic individuals.

[131] I felt I was called by this family and the situation to make the blessing; being sensitive to the unexpected nature of God's call, I felt I was just a humble instrument (SpEx 149–157).

[132] Ignatius would probably call this desolation, and the little voice is the Spirit's call to right the unbalance (SpEx 317).

[133] Alison Wertheimer, *A Special Scar: The Experiences of People Bereaved by Suicide* (Hove: Brunner-Routledge, 2001, second edition), p. 77.

[134] The restless unease, desolation, was indicating there was a problem with my highly individualistic plan and that I needed to find a way of resolving that (SpEx 317).

[135] Ignatius encourages us to ask for what we desire, to formulate our desire as prayer (SpEx 47–48).

[136] This was a taste of what Jesus experienced in his passion and crucifixion (SpEx 203).

Chapter 15

[137] The Breastplate of St Patrick: www.ourcatholicprayers.com/st-patricks-breastplate.html.

[138] 'Compostela' comes from the Latin *'Campus Stellae'* (i.e. Field of Stars). Legend has it Saint James' bones were carried from Jerusalem to northern Spain, where they were buried in a field in which later a local shepherd spotted a star. A church was built on this site, and it later became the famously beautiful Cathedral of Santiago de Compostela.

[139] This was for me a remembering of all the gifts and graces that I had received en route and I was offering myself to God in the Liturgy of the Mass (SpEx 234).

[140] The Eucharistic Prayer or 'Anaphora' is the central part of the Mass, which contains the prayer of thanksgiving and consecration of the bread and wine.

[141] At that particular time they were using the old translation of Eucharistic Prayer II; the new translation (2011) reads well also: 'Remember also our brothers and sisters who have fallen asleep in the hope of the Resurrection and all who have died in your mercy: welcome them into the light of your face.'

142 Ignatius asks us, in the third week of the Exercises, to personalise our connection with Jesus, feeling tears and grief for what he has suffered for us (SpEx 203).

143 I was deeply affected by the debate over suicide and hell (see Brendan McManus, 'Surviving Suicide').

Chapter 16

144 Of course Donal was also my deceased brother's name.

145 David Fleming, 'Prayer Is a Conversation', *Ignatian Spirituality*, www.ignatianspirituality.com/ignatian-prayer/the-spiritual-exercises/prayer-is-a-conversation.

146 Discernment for Ignatius meant examining our interior movements or moods as to whether they lead in a good or bad direction (David Fleming, *Draw Me into Your Friendship*, pp. 243–245).

147 SpEx 313–336.

148 This is another example of *agere contra*, acting against the instinct for inertia or stagnation and opening up to new possibilities (SpEx 13).

149 William Johnston (ed.), *The Cloud of Unknowing and the Book of Privy Counseling* (New York: Doubleday, 1973).

150 This is a definition of consolation, that inner movement that comes from God (SpEx 316).

151 Ignatius, in his note on doing penance, seeks to have the external act mirror the internal desire of asking God for some special favour or grace (SpEx 87). By doing penance here I brought my whole body into the act of asking God for release from this burden of grief; I committed myself fully to the prayer and the process, psychologically and now physically, in underlying my desire for God's grace.

152 Don't undo a good decision just because you experience doubts or resistance (SpEx 319).

153 Ignatius would have called this deep consolation, being on fire with God's love, and realising that everything is a freely given gift; a 'fourth week' experience (SpEx 234).

154 *A Pilgrim's Journey*, p. 31; see also Brian O'Leary, 'What New Life Is This?', *Irish Messenger*, December 2006, www.catholicireland.net/what-new-life-is-this/.

Select References and Recommended Further Reading

George Aschenbrenner, 'Consciousness Examen', *Review for Religious*, Vol. 31, No. 1, January 1972, pp. 14–21.

William A. Barry, 'Discernment: How Do I Know I'm Experiencing God?', *Ignatian Spirituality*, www.ignatianspirituality.com/making-good-decisions/discernment-of-spirits/how-do-i-know-im-experiencing-god.

deMello Spirituality Center, www.demellospirituality.com.

Tad Dunne, 'Extremism in Ignatius of Loyola', *Review for Religious*, Vol. 45, No. 3, May–June 1986, pp. 345–355.

John English, *Spiritual Freedom: From an Experience of the Ignatian Exercises to the Art of Spiritual Guidance* (Chicago, IL: Loyola Press, 1995, second edition).

Emilio Estevez (Director), *The Way*, www.theway-themovie.com.

Federación Española de Asociaciones de Amigos del Camino de Santiago, www.caminosantiago.org/cpperegrino/comun/inicio.asp.

David L. Fleming, *Draw Me into Your Friendship: The Spiritual Exercises: A Literal Translation and a Contemporary Reading of the Spiritual Exercises* (St Louis, MO: Institute of Jesuit Sources, 1996).

Thomas H. Green, *Weeds Among the Wheat* (Notre Dame, IN: Ave Maria Press, 1984).

Brian Grogan, *Alone and on Foot: Ignatius of Loyola* (Dublin: Veritas, 2008).

Michael Harter (ed.), *Hearts on Fire: Praying with Jesuits* (Chicago, IL: Loyola Press, 2005).

Gerard W. Hughes, *In Search of a Way: Two Journeys of Spiritual Discovery* (London: Darton, Longman and Todd, 1986).

Ignatian Camino, http://caminoignaciano.org/en.

Ignatian Spirituality, www.ignatianspirituality.com.

Michael Ivens (edited by Joseph Munitiz), *An Approach to Saint Ignatius of Loyola* (Oxford: Way Books, 2008).

Harold S. Kushner, *When Bad Things Happen to Good People* (New York: Anchor Books, 2004).

Brian J. Lehane, 'Attitude of Gratitude: The Examen Prayer of St. Ignatius', *Partners*, www.jesuits-chgdet.org/wp-content/uploads/2011/03/Partners_FA09.Sprituality.pdf.

Richard Leonard, *Where the Hell Is God?* (Mahwah, NJ: Paulist Press, 2010).

David Lonsdale, *Dance to the Music of the Spirit: The Art of Discernment* (London: Darton, Longman and Todd, 1992).

Chris Lowney, *Heroic Leadership* (Chicago, IL: Loyola Press, 2003).

James Martin, *The Jesuit Guide to (Almost) Everything* (New York: HarperOne, 2010).

Brendan McManus, 'Surviving Suicide', *The Furrow*, Vol. 61, No. 2, February 2010.

Brendan McManus, 'Ignatian Pilgrimage: The Inner Journey – Loyola to Manresa on Foot', *The Way*, Vol. 49, No. 3, July 2010.

Peter Muller and Angel Fernandez de Aranguiz (translated by Laurie Dennett), *Every Pilgrim's Guide to Walking to Santiago de Compostela* (Norwich: Canterbury Press, 2010).

Joseph Munitiz, 'St Ignatius of Loyola and Severe Depression', *The Way*, Vol. 44, No. 3, July 2005, pp. 58–59.

Brian O'Leary, *Ignatian Spirituality* (Dublin: Messenger Publications, 2009).

Gerard O'Mahony, *Finding the Still Point* (Guilford: Eagle Publishing, 1992).

Michael O'Sullivan, 'Trust Your Feelings but Use Your Head', *Studies in the Spirituality of Jesuits*, Vol. 22, No. 4, 1990.

Andy Otto, 'The Ignatian Way: Contemplative in Action', *God in All Things*, 19 July 2012, http://godinallthings.com/2012/ 07/19/the-ignatian-way-contemplative-in-action.

Pope Francis, *The Joy of the Gospel: Evangelii Gaudium*, Papal Encyclical (Frederick, MD: Word Among Us Press, 2014).

Richard Rohr, *Falling Upward: A Spirituality for the Two Halves of Life* (London: Society for Promoting Christian Knowledge, 2011).

Joyce Rupp, *Praying Our Goodbyes: A Spiritual Companion through Life's Losses and Sorrows* (Notre Dame, IN: Ave Maria Press, 1988).

Joyce Rupp, *Walk in a Relaxed Manner: Life Lessons from the Camino* (Maryknoll, NY: Orbis Books, 2005).

Margaret Silf, *Inner Compass: An Invitation to Ignatian Spirituality* (Chicago, IL: Loyola Press, 1998).

Joseph Tylenda, *A Pilgrim's Journey: The Autobiography of Ignatius of Loyola* (Collegeville, MN: The Order of St Benedict, 1991).

URCamino, Camino de Santiago information, www.urcamino.com.

Joseph Veale, 'The Dynamic of the Exercises', *The Way*, Supplement, Vol. 52, Spring 1985.

Alison Wertheimer, *A Special Scar: The Experiences of People Bereaved by Suicide* (Hove: Brunner-Routledge, 2001, second edition).

Mark Williams and Danny Penman, *Mindfulness: Finding Peace in a Frantic World* (New York: Rodale Books, 2011).

Monty Williams, *The Gift of Spiritual Intimacy* (Toronto, ON: Novalis, 2009).

Note: Reading the Spiritual Exercises of St Ignatius directly is a frustrating affair as they are originally written as guidelines for retreat directors who have to adapt them to persons and contexts as needed, hence they seem turgid and obscure for many readers. Instead I suggest some of the excellent guides to and interpretations of the Spiritual Exercises, such as the Fleming, O'Leary and Silf books listed above.

A Ritual for Bereavement

Based on the Camino experience, this is a suggested list of steps for someone working though a loss; ideally this process would be facilitated by a spiritual guide, director or soul friend (*anam cara*).

1. Get in touch with your deepest desire; what is it you really want at this stage in your bereavement process? To do this means in fact to place yourself in the hands of God, explicitly admitting that a solution is beyond yourself.
2. Present yourself to God in a prayer asking for the healing or grace you want, but being open to what God wants for you, e.g. 'Give me some peace of mind with this terrible grief, but not my will but yours be done.'
3. Select a symbol of the person whom you have lost, something that evokes them strongly, e.g. a piece of clothing, a photo or a personal item.
4. Set yourself some physical challenge that will stretch you. Not one that is impossible, but one that has some ascetical quality and some meditative element. Carry your symbol with you on this challenge. For example, walk to a special place, climb a mountain, swim a certain number of lengths in a pool or cycle a route that is special for you.
5. Prepare a ritual that has meaning for you, e.g. burning a piece of the person's clothing, burying a journal of your grief, refurbishing a favorite chair of your beloved, prayerfully disposing of their personal effects or honouring a special photo.
6. Afterwards, do a simple purification with water, e.g. having a long shower, a dip in a pool or a swim in the sea. Remember your

birth in the Spirit (i.e. baptism) and how you are a child of God, renewed by Christ.

7. Finally, reflect on the whole process to see where you have been moved, if there is a new freedom in you or not, or simply where God has been present. Write up your reflections in a private journal.

You may have to repeat this process a number of times, adjusting certain elements as you go. Notice where you might be getting stuck and pray for help with that part.

Ignatius of Loyola's Guidelines

Negotiating Life's Journey

Walking the road of life:

1. Remember that you are a pilgrim, just passing through life. You put yourself on the road, a journey into the unknown, to be open to hear God's call.
2. It's a pilgrim God who is always trying to find us, even in difficult situations. God is with you even if you are not with God.
3. Walking puts you in touch with your deeper desires, what you really want. These will bring us to God by following this longing.
4. Keep on track by following the signs that are only to be found in reflection and meditation. Trust your inner compass to guide you.
5. Take time out regularly to reflect on your path (i.e. Review of the Day), be flexible in progressively altering things as you go and don't be afraid of change.
6. Take time over decisions; they are important 'crossroads' moments in your life. Never make a hasty decision – rather play for time and ponder the options internally before deciding.
7. If you get lost, be humble enough to backtrack to a known, sure spot. Beware of pride driving you on, getting you even more lost.
8. Possessions are only temporary; don't hold onto things too tightly. Practice detachment: use things insofar as they are useful and discard them when they get in the way.
9. You can expect fierce storms on the road. The important thing is not to be deterred from your course but to hang on tightly to those support structures you know to be sound (prayer, discernment

and reflection). Don't change course, undo decisions or alter the structure in mid-storm.

10. Protecting yourself is important, as is having good defences against whatever comes. This means knowing your own weak spots and 'unfree' areas as this is where you are likely to be vulnerable. (Ignatius recommends fortifying your defences to anticipate challenges.)